Endorsements

In a time of global challenge, Dr. James O. Davis has given us *Living Life from a Heavenly Edge* that will inspire our faith and give us hope. The Bible tells us that "perfect love casts out fear" (1 John 4:18). But the way we know that love is through faith. This study will enhance your spiritual self-image and build your faith in God."

—Dr. Doug Beacham
General Superintendent
International Pentecostal Holiness Church

Living Life from a Heavenly Edge by Dr. James O. Davis is the quintessential book on understanding what it means to be "in Christ" and to appropriate His promises to us. Through his global leadership travels, combined with his dynamic exposition of the book of Ephesians, Dr. Davis will inspire you to believe for incredible answers to prayer in your life. Be sure to get enough copies for you and your team!

—Dr. Timothy Hill
General Overseer
Church of God, Cleveland, TN

Every life-challenge can be addressed by our faith in God and by who we are in Christ. It is paramount for Christians to grow in their faith throughout their lives. In *Living Life from a Heavenly Edge,* Dr. James O. Davis shows us the success path to fighting from victory rather than fighting for victory. When you read this powerful resource, you will be able to gain the higher ground of spiritual advantage over Satan. Every Christian leader will greatly benefit from this valuable resource!

—**Dr. Tommy Barnett**
Founder, The Dream Center
Dream Center Church

Dr. James O. Davis, in *Living Life from a Heavenly Edge*, has provided the quintessential book to help Christians to live the life of faith. Dr. Davis states, "If you please the Lord, it does not matter who you displease; but, if you displease the Lord, it does not matter who you please." Throughout this life-changing book, you will learn how to become the believer who inherits Christ's blessings and wins spiritual battles."

—**Dr. Kenneth C. Ulmer, DMin, PhD**
Faithful Central Bible Church
Global Church Divinity School

It is my privilege and joy to call Dr. James O. Davis my friend and gospel partner for twenty years. In his most recent book, *Living Life from a Heavenly Edge*, you will fortify your faith, strengthen your soul, and lift your life to new heights. When you read this book, you will find yourself soaring with wings like eagles and you will never be the same.

—**Dr. James Merritt, Lead Pastor**
Cross Point Church, Duluth, GA
President Emeritus, Southern Baptist Convention

In *Living Life from a Heavenly Edge,* Dr. James O. Davis teaches us how to live "in the heavenly places in Christ, . . . and holy and blameless before Him." You will learn what it means to live above life's circumstances and to be able to stand against satanic attacks through faith in Christ. When you read and reap from this book, your life will be enriched forever!

—**Dr. Gustavo Crocker**
General Superintendent
Church of the Nazarene

When Dr. James O. Davis writes, he writes with compassion, clarity, and conviction. *Living Life from a Heavenly Edge* is taken from one of my favorite books of the Bible for sure—the book of Ephesians. Each verse is overflowing with power-packed messages, and James brings out some of the best you'll ever read. Good foundational Bible exegesis teaching is critical for this time, and I thank James for taking the time to put this book together. I encourage everyone to pick it up and be blessed!

—**Pastor Peter Mortlock**
Senior Pastor
City Impact Churches International

Dr. James O. Davis knows how to live in the presence of God, takes steps of faith on the promises of God, and knows how to pray in the presence of God. His ministry demonstrates the truth he writes about from the book of Ephesians that he calls *Living Life from a Heavenly Edge*. I have been with Dr. Davis in South America, Africa, Europe, Asia, and the Islands of Sea, and I have seen him live and minister what he writes. So as you read this book, look beyond the words to see the heart of this man, and to experience the presence of Jesus.

—**Dr. Elmer Towns**
Cofounder/Liberty University

We are called to live our lives from a heavenly Christ-centered perspective. Too often we see this life with our human eyes and miss the blessing to see the world through God's eyes and His DESIGN for us! In his latest book, *Living Life from a Heavenly Edge*, Dr James O. Davis fully demonstrates who we are in Christ, where we are in Christ, why we are in Christ, and how we can win and overcome life's darkest moments in Christ! This powerful book is for every Christian leader who wants to live by faith a victorious Christian life!

—**Dr. Gaetano Sottile**
Italy For Christ
President and Founder

Dr. James O. Davis, in his latest book entitled *Living Life from a Heavenly Edge*, teaches us how to take the biblical steps of faith into victory. Dr. Davis walks us through a verse-by-verse study of the book of Ephesians, showing us how to believe God for the impossible to be released in our lives. I encourage you to buy a box of books and pass them out to the key leaders on your team.

—**Dr. David Sobrepena, Founder**
Word of Hope Church, Manila, Philippines
General Superintendent
Philippines Assemblies of God

Dr. James O. Davis has invested four decades into Christian leaders in 190 nations. In his latest book, *Living Life from a Heavenly Edge,* Dr. Davis expounds every verse in the book of Ephesians. This beautiful exposition will leave you embracing the truths of Paul's benediction at the conclusion of chapter 3: "Now to him who is able to do immeasurably more than all we ask or imagine, according to his power that is at work within us" (Ephesians 3:20).Take the time to read this work and allow the book of Ephesians to come alive in your life and walk of faith.

—**Dr. Carla Sunberg**
General Superintendent
Church of the Nazarene

Dr. James O. Davis' latest book, *Living Life from a Heavenly Edge*, teaches us verse-by-verse of how we should live our Christians lives through the lessons in Ephesians. In the words of St. Paul, Christ dwells in our midst, and our bodies are the temples of Christ. This history can be traced as follows: the two stone tablets, the ark, the tabernacle, the temple, birth of Jesus, resurrection and ascension, sitting on the right hand of God in heaven, sending of the Holy Spirit, Christ dwells in us, and then "your body is the temple of Christ." This book will enlighten you on the most amazing fact of how we are the temple of Christ, and how to live knowing who we are, why we are, and where we are in Christ.

—**Dr. Byoungho Zoh**
President of Bible Tongdokwon
Editor of Tongdok Bible

Living Life from a *Heavenly* EDGE

James O. Davis

Unless otherwise indicated, all Scripture quotations are taken from the *New American Standard Bible*, Copyright © The Lockman Foundation 1960, 1962, 1963, 1968, 1971, 1972, 1973, 1975, 1977, 1995. Used by permission.

Scripture quotations marked (KJV) are taken from the *King James Version* of the Bible. Public domain.

Scripture quotations marked (ESV) are taken from the *English Standard Version*, ESV® Text Edition: 2016. Copyright © 2001 by Crossway Bibles, a publishing ministry of Good News Publishers.

Scripture quotations marked (NIV) are taken from the *New International Version*®, NIV® Copyright ©1973, 1978, 1984, 2011 by Biblica, Inc.® Used by permission. All rights reserved worldwide.

Living Life from a Heavenly Edge

Copyright © 2022 by Dr. James O. Davis

ISBN: 978-0-9908371-9-0

Billion Soul Publishing
Orlando, Florida
www.billionsoulpub.com

Contents and/or cover may not be reproduced in whole or part in any form without written consent of the author.

In Dedication To

*Dr. Leonard Sweet,
who has faithfully shown the Body of Christ
how to live the Christian life
from a heavenly edge.*

*He has personally taught me
how to view life wider, value love deeper,
and to voyage with the Lord further.*

Living Life from a Heavenly Edge Ephesians Outline

Foreword xvii
Introduction 1

THE HOLY BELIEVER

I. **Who We Are in Christ**..................................... 11
   A. We Need to Recognize Our Righteousness
   B. We Need to Rely on Our Resources
   C. We Need to Rest in Our Relationship

II. **Why We Are in Christ**..................................... 23
   A. We Praise the Father Who Has Selected Us
      1. Jesus died for everyone
      2. God wants everyone to be saved
      3. The Holy Spirit convicts all people
      4. The last invitation in the Bible
   B. We Need to Praise the Son Who Saved Us
      1. We Have a Pardon in Jesus
      2. We Have a Purpose in Jesus
      3. We Have a Possession in Jesus
   C. We Need to Praise the Spirit Who Sealed Us

III. **Where We Are in Christ** 33
   A. The World Was Legally Lost
   B. The World Will Be Righteously Recovered
   C. The World Will Be Gloriously Given

THE HEAVENLY BLESSINGS

IV. Our Witness in Christ.................................. 47
    A. We Should Reflect on Our Past Guilt
    B. We Need to Recall Our Present Grace
    C. We Need to Realize Our Prospective Glory

V. Our Worship in Christ.................................. 61
    A. Spiritual Wealth for Their Needfulness
    B. Spiritual Strength for Their Weakness
    C. Spiritual Depth for Their Shallowness
    D. Spiritual Perspective for Their Narrowness
    E. Spiritual Fullness for Their Emptiness

THE HONORABLE BEHAVIOR

VI. Our Wholeness in Christ............................... 77
    A. The Ground of Our Harmony Is Truth
        1. One Body
        2. One Spirit
        3. One Hope
        4. One Lord
        5. One Faith
        6. One Baptism
        7. One God
    B. The Glory of Harmony Is Our Diversity
    C. The Goal of Harmony Is Our Maturity

VII. Our World in Christ.................................... 89
    A. The Greatness of God
    B. The Goodness of God
    C. The Grace of God

VIII. **Our Wealth in Christ** 99
    A. How the Gifts Are Delivered
    B. How the Gifts Are Described
    C. How the Gifts Are Developed
    D. How the Gifts Are Displayed

IX. **Our Wins in Christ** 113
    A. We Must Have Repentance
    B. We Must Have Resistance
    C. We Must Have Renewal

X. **Our Wage in Christ** 121
    A. The Compelling Reasons for Forgiveness
        1. The grace factor
        2. The guilt factor
        3. The grief facto
        4. The gain factor
    B. The Costly Requirements for Forgiveness
        1. Forgive freely
        2. Forgive fully
        3. Forgive finally
        4. Forgive forcefully
    C. The Certain Results of Forgiveness
        1. Personal emancipation
        2. Mutual reconciliation
        3. Spiritual rejuvenation

XI. **Our Watch in Christ** 131
    A. Time Is a Provided Opportunity
    B. Time Is a Present Opportunity
        1. Forget past guilt
        2. Forget past glory
        3. Forget past grief
        4. Forget past grudges

    C. Time Is a Precious Opportunity
       1. The Prayer Principle
       2. The Priority Principle
       3. The Promptness Principle
       4. The Power Principle
    D. Time Is a Passing Opportunity

XII. Our Will in Christ 143
    A. What Is the Answer?
       1. Education is not the answer
       2. Activism is not the answer
       3. Emotionalism is not the answer
       4. Pharisaism is not the answer
    B. A Spirit-filled Church Is the Answer
    C. What Does It Mean to be Filled with the Spirit?
       1. Continuous control by the Spirit
       2. Subjection to the Spirit
       3. Possession by a Person
    D. The Holy Spirit Has a Mind
    E. The Holy Spirit Has Emotions
    F. The Holy Spirit Has a Will

XIII. Our Wedding in Christ 153
    A. The Position of a Spirit-filled Husband
    B. The Pattern of a Spirit-filled Husband
    C. The Practice of a Spirit-filled Husband
       1. Husbands are to love wives selflessly
       2. Husbands are to love wives sacrificially
       3. Husbands are to love wives sanctifying
       4. Husbands are to love wives satisfyingly
       5. Husbands are to love wives supremely
       6. Husbands are to love wives steadfastly

XIV. **Our Way in Christ** **161**
    A. We Need to Understand the Reasons for Being Spirit-filled
        1. Our obedience.
        2. Our obligations.
            a. Our worship life
            b. Our wedded life
            c. Our work life
            d. Our war life
            e. Our witnessing life
        3. Our opportunities
    B. We Must Undertake the Requirements for Being Spirit-filled
        1. A complete commitment
        2. A continual control
        3. A conscious claiming
    C. We Must Utilize the Results of Being Spirit-filled
        1. In our relationship to God – a spirit of adoration
        2. In our relationship to circumstances – a spirit of appreciation
        3. In our relationship to people – a spirit of accommodation

XV. **Our Work in Christ** **175**
    A. We Have the Drudgery of Work
    B. We Have the Dignity in Our Work
    C. We Have the Duty of Our Work
        1. When at work, do not brag
        2. When at work, do not nag
        3. When at work, do not lag
        4. When at work, do not sag

THE HORRIFIC BATTLES

XVI. Our Warfare in Christ 189
  A. The Christian Warrior and Our Adversary
   1. Satan is a decided fact
   2. Satan is a destructive foe
   3. Satan is a defeated force
  B. The Christian and our Armor
   1. The believer's integrity
   2. The believer's purity
   3. The believer's tranquility
   4. The believer's certainty
   5. The believer's sanity
  C. The Christian and Our Attack
   1. The place of our stance
   2. The power of our sword
   3. The provision of the Spirit
  D. The Christian Warrior and Our Allies

Conclusion 201
About the Author and His Resources 205
Dr. James O. Davis Books and Resources 207

Foreword

In Ecclesiastes 7:1 we read, "The day of one's death is better than the day of one's birth." He said the day of one's death is better than the day of one's birth because life was so meaningless to him, but we can say it because we have the confident hope of heaven. When the Apostle Paul said, "For me to live is Christ and to die is gain," he voiced the same joyous and wonderful hope. And what is it that makes death joyful? What is it that makes hope joyous? It is the prospect of heaven!

Heaven is the abode of God. It is uniquely God's home. And though He is everywhere, at all times, the very unique place of His residence is heaven. Think about who and what is in heaven. Our Father is there, our Savior is now there, our fellow saints of Old Testament and New Testament times are there, the holy angels are there, our names are there, our inheritance is there, our reward is there, our treasure is there, and our citizenship is there. You are there already!

Even now, though we're not in heaven, we are living in the heavenlies. Dr. James O. Davis, in *Living Life from a Heavenly Edge,* teaches us who we are in Christ, why we are in Christ and where we are in Christ. That is, we have a foretaste of divine glory because we have the Holy Spirit dwelling in us and already see the heavenly power of God working through us. We know something of the joy of heaven, something of the love of heaven, something of the power of heaven, something of the blessedness of heaven, granted to us in Christ by the presence of the Holy Spirit who gives us love, joy, peace, gentleness, goodness, faith, meekness and self-control. All of those things in full bloom come to reality in heaven. We are aliens here and really belong to a heavenly environment. Someday, we're going to go there and live in that heavenly place, until we can truly live our lives from a heavenly edge.

We can live life from a heavenly edge, which means that we enjoy eternal life and all the blessing of the fruit of the Spirit here and now, which is a foretaste of divine glory.

I love what David said at the end of Psalm 23. David said, "Surely goodness and lovingkindness will follow me all the days of my life." And then what? "Then I will dwell in the house of the Lord." And where is the house of the Lord? Where does God dwell? He dwells in heaven. The hope of the psalmist was to be absent from the body to be present with the Lord, exactly what the Apostle Paul said in 2 Corinthians chapter 5. So whatever paradise is, it was before the resurrection and it's still after the resurrection, and the only conclusion you can make is that paradise is heaven. Until we get there, we can live life from a heavenly edge, which means that we enjoy eternal life and all the blessing of the fruit of the Spirit here and now, which is a foretaste of divine glory.

Where is heaven? Now, I want you to know heaven is a place. It's a place like New York City, in that New York City is a place. It's not a place like New York City in terms of what New York City is, it's a place like New York City in terms of the fact that New York City is somewhere—and so is heaven. It's a place like China or South America or the Alps. It is a place.

However, don't ask for a map because there are no maps. You can't chart its longitude, can't chart its latitude, it can't be located in terms of geography, and it can't be charted, even in space. Yet, it is a place. It is a place where people who have glorified bodies (like Christ's resurrection body) will actually move around and live and function forever.

Jesus, when He came out of the grave, could eat, walk, and talk. He could drink as He did at the table with His disciples. He could be touched and felt and recognized when He gave people the revelation that made Him recognizable in His glorified form. So, heaven is a place for glorified people who are real. It's a place.

You say, "Well, now, where is it?" Heaven is up. Paul says he was caught up into the third heaven, 2 Corinthians 12:2. Jesus reminded us that when He came to earth, He descended, and when He left to go back to heaven, He ascended, Ephesian 4:8-10. It's up. He came down and went back up. Now, the angels told the early disciples in Acts 1:11, "This same Jesus who is taken up from you shall so come in like manner as you've seen Him go." When the Lord returns, 1 Thessalonians 4:16 says, He will come down from heaven and we will be caught up from earth into heaven.

I Thessalonians 4:17, says we'll be caught up. When God contemplates His creatures, Psalm 53:2 says, He looks down. And when man contemplates God, according to Psalm 121:1, he looks up. When John was given a vision of heaven in Revelation 4, the Word came to him, "Come up here and I'll show you heaven." The New Jerusalem, which is the eternal dwelling place of the saints, is seen coming down out of heaven. So clearly these and other Scriptures tell us it's up.

Yet, you may ask, "Well, up where?" Up in the third heaven, and beyond space is the third heaven. It's beyond them all. You say, "Well, how far is that?" Pioneer 1, in fall of 1958, went 70,000 miles into space and didn't get to heaven. Fortunately, neither did the Soviet Lunik 1. It went up in 1959, orbited the sun, and sent back observations from 373,000 miles up, and it's not in heaven. U.S. Pioneer 4 went 407,000 miles up, and we've been sending them out further and further, and so far, none of them are in heaven. In the 1970s, Voyager 1 and 2 traveled outside of our Milky Way Galaxy, billions and billions of miles, but they have not yet reached heaven.

Heaven does not have little metal things floating around in it or satellites orbiting in it. None of them are there. You say, "Well, how far do you have to go to get there?" Well, let's think about it. The moon is 211,463 miles up. You could walk it. In theory you could walk it in 27 years if you did 24 miles a day. But when you get to the moon, you won't be in heaven. A ray of light reaches the moon in 1.5 seconds because it's going 186,000 miles a second. Now, let's just get moving at that speed and maybe we can get to heaven.

If we could go that fast, we'd be in Mercury in 4.5 minutes. It's only 50 million miles. If we were going at the speed of light, 186,000 miles a second, we'd be on Mars in 4 minutes and 21 seconds. It's only 34 million miles. We could get to Jupiter in 35 minutes and 11 seconds, because it's 367 million miles. Now, if we're going at the speed of light, we'd hit Saturn in about an hour and ten seconds. That's 790 million miles. Yet, you would not be in heaven.

Uranus (that's from the Greek word *ouranos*, which means heaven) is 1.5 billion miles. That'll take a little longer. Neptune is about three billion miles and Pluto is even further! As long as we're going, we'll just keep going. And when we got past Pluto, and we're way out there, we're still not in heaven. We haven't gotten there yet!

Now, let me give it to you from another perspective. Our Earth is one of nine planets revolving around the sun. I realize many scientists no longer call Pluto a planet, but I still do. Our Earth has a diameter of 8,000 miles. Its mass is estimated to be six septillion, six hundred sextillion tons. So, we're in this massive, heavy thing, spinning around about 211,000 miles to the moon and about 93 million miles to the sun. The sun, by the way, has a diameter of 866,500 miles and a mass 330,000 times larger than the earth.

When you start expanding your mind through all these numbers and moving out into the galaxy, you just can't contain yourself.

The sun is one star in a galaxy of some 100 billion other stars. And we're still in just our little part of the universe. Distances, again, become so great that they can't be measured in terms of miles. They must be measured in lightyears, which is 186,000 miles a second or 11,160,000 miles a minute. The sun is eight light minutes away.

When you start expanding your mind through all these numbers and moving out into the galaxy, you just can't contain yourself. For example, our solar system has a diameter of 660 light minutes. Yet, this galaxy is a very small part with a diameter of 100,000 lightyears. And get this: There are 500 billion galaxies. You say, "I'm beginning to feel like heaven is a long way away." That's right!

Now get this: Jesus said to the thief on the cross. "Today, you will be with me in paradise." Now, that is fast. You say, "How can that be?" I don't know. Paul was caught up and didn't know what was going on. He says, "I don't know whether I was in my body, out of my body or anything, I just know I was caught up to the third heaven and back again the same day." How can that be?

The Bible says it's so fast that you will be changed in the what? Twinkling of an eye. That doesn't mean a blink, that means the time it takes for light to flash off your pupil. That's fast. We will be moving so fast, it's inconceivable. Heaven is up, and heaven is far, but heaven is near! You say, "How do we understand that?" We don't understand it. Heaven is huge. You need to know that. It's huge. How big is heaven? Are you ready for this? As big as God. You say, "How big is God?" He's infinite.

Heaven is up and beyond everything that we know in the material universe. It is as big as God.

You see, wherever our universe ends, the universe as we know it, the time-and-space universe, it is surrounded by infinite, eternal heaven. So, heaven isn't just up there, heaven is the infinity of the presence of God that surrounds the almost endless universe. It's incredible. It encircles our universe and is as big as our God.

Heaven is up and beyond everything that we know in the material universe. It is as big as God. It is that which engulfs within it the material universe as we know it, which is billions and billions of lightyears to its extensions. Now, we can't keep thinking about that because once we have gotten beyond the universe, the universe of time and space as we know it, is infinity. And it is as infinite as God is infinite and that's how infinite heaven is. We can't handle it because we are captive to a time/space mentality. We cannot conceive of endless, eternal heaven. Yet, think about it: As Christians we are on earth, but at the same time we are seated with Christ in the heavenlies. We are in the "earthlies" and the heavenlies at the same time.

When we were regenerated, justified, converted, Christ came to be in us. This is a profound reality and is the distinguishing characteristic of Christianity and the whole power and motive of our sanctification. In Ephesians 2:3, Paul says, "Blessed be the God and Father of our Lord Jesus Christ, who has blessed us with every spiritual blessing in the heavenlies"—or heavenly places—"in Christ." Now the operative phrase is "in Christ." Every spiritual blessing that heaven possesses to grant is in Christ.

Apart from Christ there are no heavenly blessings. There is no other name by which you may be saved. Apart from Christ, heaven gives you nothing but judgment and wrath. There is no way to tap any heavenly blessings unless you are in Christ. Apart from Christ, there is only condemnation and judgment. Everything is in Christ. In Ephesians 2:6, Paul writes "seated," not "will seat." The tense is significant. What happened on the first Ascension Day involved us no less than Christ.

How can this be? Only because we are "in Christ" (Ephesians 2:6-7). This is not an easy concept to get our heads around, but it's central to living life from a heavenly edge. Trying to be literal about all this won't help us understand it. How can every one of us who is in Christ be seated with Christ? It was crowded enough at the Last Supper! Drawing up a tentative seating plan for "the heavenly places" won't help either.

Nor will misunderstanding the idea of sitting. For some, sitting conjures up sitting in a chair or sitting on the floor. That's not the sitting that Paul has in mind. To be seated with the exalted Christ is to enjoy a position of privilege. You'll remember that James and John asked to sit, one at the right hand and one at the left hand of Christ in his glory (Mark 10:35-37). Paul tells us that every last one of us who is in Christ, however insignificant we may think we are, gets to enjoy this privilege, not just in some distant future, but now.

Since we are seated with the ascended Christ, we enjoy immediate access to God in prayer. We're speaking to the God who has already seated us beside him in Christ and now waits to hear what we have to say.

Some wonderful things flow from being seated in Christ in heavenly places. Paul says that God's purpose in seating us in the heavenly places was so that "he might show the immeasurable riches of his grace in kindness toward us in Christ Jesus" (Ephesians 2:7). We are not at a vast distance, waiting for some promised kindness that has yet to materialize. In Christ, we have already been welcomed into God's immediate presence; we have already been seated at God's table like a son or daughter; we have already been given a place of honor; and God's purpose in all this is to shower us, even as we complete our lives on earth, with his immeasurable kindness.

Since we are seated with the ascended Christ, we enjoy immediate access to God in prayer. We're not speaking from our small place on earth into a distant silence in the hope that God might perhaps hear. We're speaking to the God who has already seated us beside him in Christ and now waits to hear what we have to say. In the ascended Christ, we are already seated in the very presence of God and need only turn to God and speak to Him.

While you read, *Living Life from a Heavenly Edge*, Dr. Davis will, on the one hand, enrich your life with the images and metaphors that the Apostle Paul used to communicate the privileges and promises we have as children of God. On the other hand, he will enlarge your faith to know that we do not fight in this life for victory, but we fight everyday, from victory. We are not working to win; we have already won in Christ. Dr. Davis and I have been friends for decades and it is a joy to prepare this foreword for you!

Rev. Doug Clay
General Superintendent, Assemblies of God
Springfield, Missouri

December, 2021

Introduction

How far can you see? In other words, what is your view? How far are you willing to go? In other words, what voyage will you take? What is your high ground? In other words, what is your vantage point? How high is it? We are not called to fight *for* victory, but to fight *from* victory.

On February 14, 1990, a photograph of a Pale Blue Dot was taken by NASA's Voyager 1 at a distance of 3.7 billion miles from the Sun. The image inspired the title of scientist Carl Sagan's book, "Pale Blue Dot: A Vision of the Human Future in Space." This was Voyager 1's last photo before departing our galaxy.

Voyager 1 was speeding out of the solar system—beyond Neptune when mission managers commanded it to look back toward home for a final time. It snapped a series of 60 images that were used to create the first "family portrait" of our solar system. The picture that would become known as the Pale Blue Dot shows Earth within a scattered ray of sunlight. Voyager 1 was so far away that—from its vantage point—Earth was just a point of light about a pixel in size.

In addition to Earth, Voyager 1 captured images of Neptune, Uranus, Saturn, Jupiter, and Venus. A few key members didn't show up in the shot: Mars was obscured by scattered sunlight bouncing around in the camera, Mercury was too close to the Sun, and dwarf planet Pluto was too tiny, too far away and too dark to be detected.

The images gave humans an awe-inspiring and unprecedented view of their home world and its neighbors. Like Earth, each planet appears as just a speck of light. Finding a way to display the images and capture the sheer scale of Voyager's accomplishment proved challenging. NASA's Jet Propulsion Laboratory—which built and manages the Voyager probes—mounted the entire mosaic on a wall in its Theodore von Kármán Auditorium and it covered over 20 feet.

The family portrait remains the first and only time a spacecraft has attempted to photograph our home solar system.

The family portrait remains the first and only time a spacecraft has attempted to photograph our home solar system. Only three spacecraft have been capable of making such an observation from such a distance: Voyager 1, Voyager 2 and New Horizons. Voyager 1 was launched Sept. 5, 1977, just days after its twin—Voyager 2—on Aug. 20. Because it was on a faster route to the mission's first encounter, at Jupiter, Voyager 1 overtook Voyager 2 on Dec. 15, 1977. (This was the reason for the order of their naming.) Voyager 1 flew past Jupiter on March 5, 1979, and Saturn on Nov. 12, 1980.

After snapping the Pale Blue Dot and other "family photos,"—at 05:22 GMT, Feb. 14, 1990—Voyager 1 powered off its cameras forever. Mission planners wanted to save its energy for the long journey ahead. In August 2012, Voyager 1 entered interstellar space. It's now the most distant human-made object ever.

NASA's Voyager 1 spacecraft is currently over 14.1 billion miles from Earth. It's moving at a speed of approximately 38,000 miles per hour and not long ago passed through our solar system's boundary with interstellar

INTRODUCTION

space. Despite that incredible distance, the spacecraft is still able to relay data back to Earth, and new discoveries are still being made.

Do you recall our opening three questions? What is your view? What is your voyage? What is your vantage? I believe when Christians learn to synergistically combine view, voyage and vantage, they will have victory!

Only three spacecraft have been capable of making such an observation from such a distance: Voyager 1, Voyager 2 and New Horizons.

Due to the Earth being round, its convexity limits the distance that is visible. The line of vision of a person of six feet in height for example would be 3.24 miles, whereas a pigeon flying at an altitude of 1 mile would command a view of 96.10 miles in every direction. If you were looking at a distant object of 44 feet in height, such as a flag on a masthead, then the flag would seem to be on the horizon, 9.35 miles away. View, voyage and vantage are so powerful when combined together. With this combined power comes perspective. We need to take the long look instead of the short look.

In the opening scenes of the movie "Gettysburg," the film adaptation of the brilliant Civil War novel "Killer Angels," Union Brig. Gen. John Buford gazes across the rolling Southern Pennsylvania hills and laments the plodding tactics of his commanders. Imagining the battle to come as an inevitable failure, he says: "When our people get here, Lee will have the high ground and there will be the devil to pay."

Buford did not wait for orders from above. Seizing the high ground for the Union, he turned the tables on the Confederates such that it was the Union, and not Lee, that held the high ground and the rocks when the battle began in earnest. Thus it was Lee, and not the Union, whose forces withered and lost the ensuing battle. The war—and the preeminent place the United States has held in the world ever since—may well have hinged on that decision.

The quest for the high ground is as old as war itself. A castle on a hill was harder to attack and provided the early warning to spot marauders while they were still a long way off.

The quest for the high ground is as old as war itself. A castle on a hill was harder to attack and provided the early warning to spot marauders while they were still a long way off. Attacking from on high offered other advantages, including speed and range, factors that remain critical even today. Manned flight—from balloons and dirigibles to powered flight in and beyond the atmosphere—take that concept to its natural conclusions.

Let's go a step further. "Spacepower," is the foundational doctrine of the U.S. Space Force. In it, the new military branch defines space as "a critical manifestation of the high ground in modern warfare"—one might even say the ultimate high ground. Providing a God's-eye view of the world beneath, legal, permission-free overflight, and the means to move and manage information globally at unparalleled speed, space is transformational.

America does not own this high ground outright. In order to gain high ground, one has to take it and keep it.

INTRODUCTION

The Space Force's objective, according to the doctrine, is to ensure the freedom to operate where, when, and how we wish; to enable the remainder of the Joint Force with precision, strategic warning, and global communications, and the ability to provide—independent of the other services—military options in, from, and to space.

Providing a God's-eye view of the world beneath, legal, permission-free overflight, and the means to move and manage information globally at unparalleled speed, space is transformational.

In order to win this high ground, the Space Force envisions five core competencies: 1) **Security**, to ensure a stable operating environment for both military and civilian space activities; 2) **Strength,** combat power to enable offensive and defensive actions to deter aggression and fight and win if necessary; 3) **Systems** for mobility and logistics, to enable movement of people and equipment in space; 4) **Statistics**, to ensure timely data collection and transmission; and 5) **Substance,** to ensure effective identification and understanding of activity in space.

When we choose to take the high ground and plan to keep it, we must think differently, believe divinely and act decisively. The winning plan for mountain top victory is not the same as valley life. Yet, so many Christians believe we obtain high-ground victory without making serious necessary changes in order to get there.

Think about the Space Force plan. First, after the voyage to space, stability is required to stay in space. Without it, success will not be short lived. Once we have decided that we are going to *Live Life from a Heavenly Edge*, we have to learn how to walk it out daily or we will ultimately fail. Second, in order to keep the high ground of space, strength is required in combat against our enemies. Just because we are first to obtain the high ground, does not mean that enemies will not try to claim it for themselves. The same is also true in the spiritual heavenlies. Once we have decided by faith to live our lives from a heavenly perspective, we will need the strength required not only to win the day but also to keep the peace every day.

Once we have decided by faith to live our lives from a heavenly perspective, we will need the strength required not only to win the day but also to keep the peace every day.

Third, once we ascend to the high ground, we have to have systems to manage our success. This is extremely important. There are no problems too big to solve, just too many small minds trying to solve them. We have to think and pray from a heavenly perspective, looking down at the earth, rather than looking up at the stars. Fourth, without up-to-date statistics, we will not be able to remain on the cutting edge very long. Life is not lived in a vacuum, neither is space. When it comes to living life from a heavenly edge, one can never have enough divine information. The right information leads to righteous inspiration!

Fifth, substance or knowledge is key to keeping the victory on higher ground. We need space-awareness above the earth, but Savior-awareness from the heavens. We need to know who we are and where we are to bring about the spiritual leverage needed to defeat Satan and his emissaries.

INTRODUCTION

As we embark on our study of the Book of Ephesians, we should remind ourselves of our opening questions: 1) How far can you see? Remember; the higher you go, the further you can see. Why should we settle for the view from Mount Everest, when we can view the world from the edge of the heavens; 2) How far are you willing to go? I am completely convinced, the more we are willing to learn, the further we can go. When you read Living *Life from a Heavenly Edge*, you are able to do more than sit on the top of the earth, dangling your feet off the edge. You will be able to wage war and win on the earth, because you have obtained the higher heavenly ground; 3) What is your vantage point? When you are driving your car, looking through your front window, you have a clear view down the road. However, if you take that same size piece of glass and change it into a window for an airplane that flies at 39,000 feet, your view from that window is completely different from a car. It is the same piece of glass, but the vantage point has been forever altered. If you learn that when you were saved, you were also placed in the heavenlies, not only will your view be greater, but victory will be sweeter! We need view, voyage, vantage and victory.

THE HOLY BELIEVER

1

Who We Are In Christ

When I was twelve years old, I received a set of barbells for Christmas. I had really wanted this gift! When I opened the package, I remember my Dad saying, "I see this is 120 pounds. That ought to keep you busy for a while." I thought to myself, "I'll show you!"

Year after year I continued to work out. I worked certain body parts on Monday, Wednesday, and Friday and other body parts on Tuesday, Thursday, and Saturday. I made sure that I ate right and got the perfect amount of protein every day! By the time I was twenty years old, I was bench-pressing 305 pounds five times and throwing 225 pounds over my head without a problem. I could curl 80-pound barbells and do triceps work with more than 100 pounds with each arm!

There came a day when we heard the news that there was going to be an arm wrestling championship at Bel Air

Mall in Mobile, Alabama. At the time, we lived about 15 miles from the mall. On a particular Saturday morning, my Dad, brother, and I went to the championship; and I decided I would enter. I did not have a lot of confidence that I would win but believed I was strong enough to go several rounds with different brutes.

The key to living a victorious Christian life is in discovering who you are in Christ.

I remember walking onto the stage and taking my position. Then it came time for me to lock hands with my opponent. The referee placed his hands on our locked hands, went over the rules, and stated, "When I let go, the arm wrestling match will begin." In took less than two seconds for my opponent to beat me! It happened so fast I didn't even know what had happened to me. This guy went on to beat everyone! He was not much to look at and did not have bulging muscles, but he knew how to win. I was so humiliated.

As we begin our journey to *live a life from a heavenly edge,* we need to comprehend from the start what real humility is. Many do not understand genuine, biblical humility and think it is going around with a hangdog expression, having an inferiority complex, and saying, "Well, I am just no good." However, we are somebody and need to develop true humility and have a true understanding of who we are and what God says about us.

> *Paul, an apostle of Christ Jesus by the will of God, To the saints who are at Ephesus and who are faithful in Christ Jesus: Grace to you and peace from God our Father and*

the Lord Jesus Christ. Blessed be the God and Father of our Lord Jesus Christ, who has blessed us with every spiritual blessing in the heavenly places in Christ, just as He chose us in Him before the foundation of the world, that we would be holy and blameless before Him. In love He predestined us to adoption as sons through Jesus Christ to Himself, according to the kind intention of His will, to the praise of the glory of His grace, which He freely bestowed on us in the Beloved (Ephesians 4:1-6).

The key to living a victorious Christian life is in discovering who you are in Christ. Many Christians have never really discovered who they are. I want you to find out who you are in the Lord Jesus Christ.

If you look at the margins of different people's Bibles — where they have been thumbed the most, marked up the most, and underlined the most, you will likely find they are in what we call the behavioral passages.

Ephesians 6 tells us how to put on the whole armor of God and how to fight and overcome. Romans 12 tells us things to do and not to do while the Beatitudes tell us how to live and how to act. These verses are behavioral passages. We study these kinds of passages over and over, but we must learn that Christianity is not behavior modification. God does not work from the outside in; He does not modify our behavior in order to change us but changes us in order to modify our behavior.

It has been said that "you'll never purify the water by painting the pump, and you're not going to purify your life by outward modification. If you try to, what you're going to end up with is legalism, and that is deadly."

The overarching outline of the book of Ephesians is as follows:

- In Chapter 1, we learn about the **holy believer**. We need to know "who" we are in Christ.
- In Chapters 2 and 3, we learn about our **heavenly blessings**. We need to know "how" we got to be who we are in Christ.
- In Chapters 4 through 6:9, we learn about our **honorable behaviors**. Paul tells us how to live like who we are in Christ.
- In Chapter 6:10-24, we learn about our **horrific battles**. Paul tells us how to prepare like we are in Christ.

It matters not how true the truth is nor how many wonderful truths there are in the Bible for they will not liberate or set you free until you personally know those truths.

If you just simply start in the practical, you will get into legalism. You will be frustrated and will try to live in a way that is not going to work out. It is frustrating to live contrary to an identity you do not have in your heart and in your mind.

Jesus said, *You will know the truth, and the truth will make you free* (John 8:32). It is truth that frees us, but what exactly is truth? Truth is whatever God says, and that truth is embodied in the Lord Jesus Christ. However, the truth does not free you until you know it.

It matters not how true the truth is nor how many wonderful truths there are in the Bible for they will not liberate or set you free until you personally know those truths. You must know the doctrinal before it can translate into the practical.

Unfortunately, many Christians do not understand the truth. They do not know who they are in Christ and have never really understood their self-image. Since they do not know what they have in Christ, they are never, ever really liberated. Spiritually, they have a lid on their minds and say, "I cannot do this. I cannot be free. I cannot succeed. I am chained by this habit. I am chained by this failure. I am chained by my limited knowledge." It is not true; but if we believe it to be true, it may as well be so.

Many Christians need to understand that they sometimes have a perception of themselves that is not true.

Many Christians need to understand that they sometimes have a perception of themselves that is not true. They believe it to be true; therefore, they are never set free. The truth is what God says, not what you think about it. What God says is true no matter how you feel about it. It is true if God says it; but it will never set you free until you know the truth.

There are several spiritual facts to learn that will liberate you. These spiritual facts will give you a proper self-image to understand what God says about you. This truth will set you free and give you a self-image that is healthy with true humility.

We Need to Recognize Our Righteousness

Paul, an apostle of Christ Jesus by the will of God, To the saints who are at Ephesus and who are *faithful in Christ Jesus* (Ephesians 1:1).

If you are in Christ Jesus, if you have received Christ as your personal Savior, if you have repented of your sins and trusted Christ, and if you have been saved, you are a saint!

Some Christians cannot attain victory because they do not understand or accept what God says — not only about their being cleansed of their sins when they were lost but also about becoming saints now that they are saved by His blood.

Our Catholic friends periodically take individuals who have achieved certain things in their Christian lives and canonize them or make them saints. However, no one can make you a saint because you are already a saint. There are only two classes of people in the world — the saints and the ain'ts.

The word "saint" means "sanctified one," one whom God has made righteous and set aside for Himself.

What is humility? You may say, "Well, you know, I just don't think I ought to call myself a saint." Real humility is accepting what God says about you. It is not what you think about it but what God says about you.

Some Christians cannot attain victory because they do not understand or accept what God says — not only about their being cleansed of their sins when they were lost but also about becoming saints now that they are saved by His blood. Victory comes when they cease to resist the idea and accept the fact that they are saints.

God calls you a saint; and you respond by saying, "Well, you mean I'm supposed to be sinless?" No, you cannot be sinless, but you can be blameless.

> *Just as He chose us in Him before the foundation of the world, that we would be holy and blameless before Him* (Ephesians 1:4).

Each of us ought to be blameless before the Lord Jesus Christ as we are saints of God. You say, "But I'm not perfect." That makes no difference. In God's sight, you are His saint.

Every one of us in some way or another has failed from time to time. If you have repented of your sin and trusted Jesus Christ to save you, you are righteous in God's sight and are a saint of God. However, until you see who you are, you are not going to behave as you ought. Your behavior comes out of the conception of who you are; and when you see that you are the righteousness of God in Christ, then you are going to begin to behave that way.

We Need to Rely on Our Resources

> *Blessed be the God and Father of our Lord Jesus Christ, who has blessed us with every spiritual blessing in the heavenly places in Christ* (Ephesians 1:3).

Not only are you righteous in God's sight and not only does God call you a saint, but God has also given you everything you need to live a Christian life.

The question is, "Who is right? You or God?" According to Ephesians 1:3, you have everything you need to live the Christian life: all the love, all the patience, all of the faith, and all of the wisdom. You might say, "If I have it, why don't I have it?" Because you have not understood that you have it. You do not have a conception of yourself as having it. You do not perceive yourself as having it. You are like the elephant that is being held by a little peg. You are like the person whose face has been changed but has never changed on the inside; therefore, you still see yourself as being without wisdom, without love, without patience, without faith, and without strength. You conceive of yourself that way; and because you conceive of yourself that way, you live that way.

God does not ask or demand anything of you that He has not already given you. God does not ask you to manufacture anything. It is already yours in Christ according to Ephesians 1:3. God has already blessed you with all spiritual blessings in heavenly places in Christ Jesus.

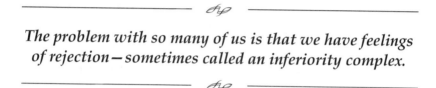

The problem with so many of us is that we have feelings of rejection—sometimes called an inferiority complex.

Truth is believing what God says—not what you think. When you understand what God says, when you understand the truth, the truth will set you free. In order to have a healthy self-image, you must recognize your righteousness in God's sight. You are a saint.

God has imputed righteousness to you, and you are the righteousness of God in Christ. God has imputed that righteousness and will never impute sin to you. That does not mean He will not carry you to the woodshed and chasten the daylights out of you if you disobey Him, but He will never put that sin on your account. One-half of one sin would damn you forever if you ever had that sin imputed to you.

How does it come? Through the knowledge of Him who called you to glory and virtue. God has already given you all things that pertain to life and godliness, everything you need to live the Christian life. You do not need anything else. How does it come? Through the knowledge of Him who has called you.

You will know the truth, and the truth will set you free. When you understand who you are in Christ Jesus and recognize your righteousness, God calls you a saint. It is not until you know this that you begin to have a healthy self-image and understand who you are in the Lord Jesus Christ.

We Need to Rest in Our Relationship

To the praise of the glory of His grace, which He freely bestowed on us in the Beloved (Ephesians 1:6).

What is your relationship? It is one of acceptance, not merely that you have accepted God but also that He has made you accepted in the Beloved.

Who is the Beloved? Jesus and you in Christ. What is true about Jesus is true about you. When God the Father looked over the battlements of heaven when the Lord Jesus was being baptized, He said, *This is My beloved Son, in whom I am well-pleased* (Matthew 3:17). If you are in Him, you are accepted in Him—in the Beloved, in the Lord Jesus.

The problem with so many of us, the reason we do not have a good self-image, the reason we have such a warped personality and psyche is that we have feelings of rejection—sometimes called an inferiority complex. Why do we have it? It is inbred; it is incipient in humanity.

Why do you think kids leave a good home where they have a nice soft bed and carpets on the floors with good clean clothes to wear and the love of a father and a mother to go live in a commune with a bunch of unwashed, unruly kids and eat sardines, potted meat, and crackers and sleep on a dirty mattress? Because in the commune, they have a feeling of being accepted.

Everyone dresses a certain way to be accepted. The world tells us if we do not use the right kind of toothpaste, or wear designer clothes, or have the right little animal on our shirt pocket, we will not be accepted. This rejection is enforced.

God does not change you in order to love you;
He loves you in order that He might change you.

Children—even little kids—can be cruel. When you were in grade school, someone may have come up to you and said, "Did you know that your ears stick out?" If you lock in on that one, you will never look in the mirror again without studying your ears. Or perhaps they said, "Did you know that one of your nostrils is bigger than the other?" Afterwards, you go through life saying, "Boy, I'd be a pretty good-looking guy if one nostril were not bigger than the other." You just want to be accepted—to be a part, and yet we have this inborn rejection.

What happens is that many Christians still have this need for acceptance. Even after they get saved, they fail to understand they are now accepted in the Beloved; consequently, they get into legalism to try to be accepted when they have already been accepted. Many Christians work hard to make God love them, thinking, "Boy, if I could just give more money . . . if I could just be at the church more . . . if I could just pray harder . . . if I could just study . . . if I could just memorize more verses, maybe then God would love me. Maybe then God would accept me."

I want to give you what I consider to be one of the greatest truths: God does not change you in order to love you; He loves you in order that He might change you.

When you are able to see that God already loves you—loves you now even though you are imperfect, even though in your own stature there are faults and failures and foibles, you are the righteousness of God in Christ. That righteousness has been imputed to you, and you need to recognize your righteousness and rely upon His resources. God has blessed you with all spiritual blessings in heavenly places in Christ Jesus. You need not only to understand this but also to receive the relationship which is that you are accepted in the Beloved and you need to quit trying to work your way to God. Holiness is not the way to Christ; Christ is the way to holiness.

The key to all of this is the phrase, "in Christ Jesus":

*Paul, an apostle of Jesus Christ by the will of God, to the saints who are at Ephesus and who are **faithful in Christ Jesus**. Grace be to you and peace, from God our Father and the Lord Jesus Christ. Blessed be the God and Father of our Lord Jesus Christ, who has blessed us with every spiritual blessing in the heavenly places in Christ, just as He chose us in Him before the foundation of the world, that we would be holy and blameless before Him. In love He predestined us to adoption as sons through Jesus Christ to Himself, according to the kind intention of His will, to the praise of the glory of His grace, which He freely bestowed on us in the Beloved* (Ephesians 1:1-6, emphasis added).

What does it mean to be in Christ? If you were to be put in a barrel, you would be in a barrel. If the barrel were to be put in the Mississippi River, you would be in the Mississippi River. If you are in a barrel, you are in a barrel; and if the barrel is put in the river, you are in a barrel in the river, correct?

Where are you now? In Christ. Where is Christ? Seated in the heavenlies. Where are you? Seated in the heavenlies. What is true about Christ is true about you. He is already enthroned and seated in the heavenlies, and all things are beneath His feet. When you understand who you are in Christ, you will have a good personality and an incredible self-image. It will not be pride but genuine humility. Humility is accepting what God says. You will know the truth, and the truth will set you free!

Why We Are in Christ

When your prayers get dry, begin to pray; they will get juicy again. When you are feeling low, pull some of the groans out of your plans and shove in a few hallelujahs; you will see it pick you up. When you run out of things to pray about, begin to praise; you will have an ocean to swim in. When it seems that God is not near, begin to praise Him; He will invade your world.

In Ephesians 1:3-14, Paul writes the most all-inclusive statement of the Gospel in the entire Bible. First, there is praise to the Father and then there is a refrain. Second, there is praise to the Son and then there is a refrain. Third, there is praise to the Holy Spirit and then there is a refrain.

The refrains are: *To the praise of the glory of his grace...* (v.6 KJV); *That we should be to the praise of his glory...* (v.12 KJV); *unto the praise of his glory* (v.14 KJV). Each time Paul states a truth about the Trinity, he then encourages us to praise Him! There are several praising steps to the heavenlies.

We Praise the Father Who Has Selected Us

> *Blessed* be *the God and Father of our Lord Jesus Christ, who has blessed us with every spiritual blessing in the heavenly* places *in Christ, just as He chose us in Him before the foundation of the world, that we would be holy and blameless before Him* (Ephesians 1:3-4).

God *chose us in Him before the foundation of the world* (Ephesians 1:4.) Before God scooped out the seas, piled up the mountains, and flung out the sun, moon, and stars, He had us in His heart and His mind.

When the Bible says, "We're chosen in Him" (Ephesians 1:4), it is not the choice of one sinner above another sinner. God is not saying, "This man is predestined for hell and this man is predestined for heaven." Anybody who wants to be saved can be saved.

Following are four major reasons why anybody who wants to be saved can be saved:

Jesus Died for Everyone

> *And He Himself is the propitiation* [the satisfaction, the atonement, the payment, the expiation] *for our sins; and not for ours only, but also for those of the whole world* (1 John 2:2).

> *When Jesus died, He died for the sins of the world. When John the Baptist saw Jesus coming, he said, Behold, the Lamb of God, who takes away the sin of the world!* (John 1:29).

God Wants Everyone to Be Saved

This is good and acceptable in the sight of God our Savior, who desires all men to be saved and to come to the knowledge of the truth (1 Timothy 2:3-4).

The Lord is not slow about His promise, as some count slowness, but is patient toward you, not wishing for any to perish but for all to come to repentance (2 Peter 3:9).

The Holy Spirit Convicts All People

And He, when He comes, will convict the world concerning sin and righteousness and judgment (John 16:8).

There was the true Light which, coming into the world, enlightens every man (John 1:9).

The Last Invitation in the Bible

The Spirit and the bride say, "Come." And let the one who hears say, "Come." And let the one who is thirsty come . . . Do you want God? He wants you. Then he wraps it up, the last invitation in the Bible . . . *let the one who wishes take the water of life without cost* (Revelation 22:17).

We were chosen—selected of God—not that He predestined some to be lost and some to be saved, but we were in the heart and mind and bosom of God before the foundation of the world. It is His choice of us that enables us to make our choice of Him.

Why did he choose us? *He predestined us to adoption as sons through Jesus Christ to Himself* (Ephesians 1:5). It gets even better; not only are we chosen, but we are also predestined.

*It is His choice of us that enables us
to make our choice of Him.*

Predestination again deals with God's children—those who are predestined or those who are chosen are predestined to be His children to be adopted into His family. Are we born into the family of God or adopted into the family of God? The answer is yes and yes. There are many other verses that speak of our being born of the Spirit and of water and being born of the Word of God. We are sons and daughters by a twofold process.

We are born into the family of God when we repent of our sins and receive Jesus Christ as our personal Savior. A miracle takes place on the inside, and we are born again. Therefore, we share His nature and are next of kin to the deity and next of kin to the Trinity. We share the very nature of God, and the God who chose us *predestined us to adoption as sons* (Ephesians 1:5).

It is thrilling when we think of what the Father has done for us, and this is the reason that Paul said, *To the praise of the glory of His grace, which He freely bestowed on us in the Beloved* (Ephesians 1:6).

We are accepted in the Beloved (Ephesians 1:6). We are in Christ and have acceptance before God. We have the same acceptance before God that Jesus Christ has before His Father!

We Need to Praise the Son Who Saved Us

In the second stanza of this marvelous hymn of praise, Paul writes about the Son who has saved us:

> *To the praise of the glory of His grace, which He freely bestowed on us in the Beloved. In Him we have redemption through His blood, the forgiveness of our trespasses, according to the riches of His grace which He lavished on us. In all wisdom and insight He made known to us the mystery of His will, according to His kind intention which He purposed in Him with a view to an administration suitable to the fullness of the times,* that is, *the summing up of all things in Christ, things in the heavens and things on the earth. In Him also we have obtained an inheritance, having been predestined according to His purpose who works all things after the counsel of His will, to the end that we who were the first to hope in Christ would be to the praise of His glory* (Ephesians 1:6–12).

As we think about the Son who saved us, we will be stretched to comprehend the redemption and riches of our salvation.

We Have a Pardon in Jesus

He speaks of the *redemption through His blood* (Ephesians 1:7) and of the *forgiveness of our trespasses* (Ephesians 1:7). Thank God for the rich, royal, ruby red blood of the Lord Jesus Christ. We are redeemed by His blood. Without the shedding of blood, there is no remission of sin. Jesus was crucified on a cruel Roman cross and experienced excruciating, unfathomable pain that we might be saved.

He not only redeemed us with His blood but also forgave our sins. In the Old Testament when they would have the Day of Atonement, the high priest would take two goats—one goat would be slain and the blood of that goat would have its blood poured out on the altar as a sacrifice for sin.

God has a plan, and that plan will not be stopped. We are on course to knowing Jesus Christ in the fullness of time.

The high priest would take the other goat and would lay his hands on its head and confess the sins of the people over the head of that goat. That goat was called a scapegoat. The sins would be put on that goat, and that goat would be led out in the wilderness and would be let go—never to return. The idea of forgiveness literally means to "bear away."

As far as the east is from the west, so far has He removed our transgressions from us (Psalm 103:12). It is impossible to measure the distance between the East and the West which is how far God has removed our sins from us. God *will cast all their sins into the depths of the sea* (Micah 7:19).

The Apostle Paul praises the Father who selected us: *He chose us in Him before the foundation of the world* (Ephesians 1:4) and praises the Son who has saved us and give us redemption and forgiveness. Our Lord has pardoned us!

We Have a Purpose in Jesus

Those who know the Lord Jesus Christ are the only ones who truly understand where they are going, the only ones who understand what this world is all about, and the only ones who can make rhyme or reason out of this world. They hold the key that unlocks the mystery of history.

> *He made known to us the mystery of His will, according to His kind intention which He purposed in Him with a view to an administration suitable to the fullness of the times,* that is, *the summing up of all things in Christ, things in the heavens and things on the earth* (Ephesians 1:9-10).

God has a plan, and that plan will not be stopped. We are on course to knowing Jesus Christ in the fullness of time. Jesus is never ahead of time and never late. He is going to harmonize everything.

Almost everyone in our current culture is totally stressed out. However, more than a hundred years ago when a person missed a stagecoach, they would say, "Well, there will be another one along in a couple of months." Yet we get all bent out of shape if we miss a section in a revolving door. The world is all stressed out with no place to go.

Why is there so much stress today? Because we are still awaiting the fulfillment of God's promise of eternal life free from pain, disappointment, sorrow, and stress. The devil and sin have not yet been cast into hell, Jesus has not yet returned to establish His kingdom on the earth, and the Church has not yet been gathered to her bridegroom — Jesus Christ.

However, God is working on a plan called "Jesus in the fullness of time." There is coming a time when everything is going to be in tune with Jesus and with everything else as well. Heaven will be in tune with earth, the spiritual will be in tune with the material, God will be in tune with man, and man will be in tune with man.

In Christ, we have been pardoned and have a purpose; but Paul is not finished.

We Have a Possession in Jesus

> *Also we have obtained an inheritance, having been predestined according to His purpose who works all things after the counsel of His will* (Ephesians 1:11).

Presently, we have a down payment that Paul calls a *pledge of our inheritance* (Ephesians 1:14). This down payment is the Holy Spirit in our hearts. In the future, we will receive our full inheritance. The riches of His grace will become the riches of His glory.

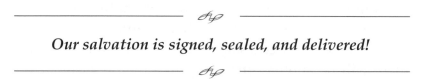

Our salvation is signed, sealed, and delivered!

We were adopted into the family of God which is why we are called *heirs of God and fellow heirs with Christ* (Romans 8:17). A fellow heir is one who will share and share alike.

Jesus has saved us and given us a pardon, a purpose, and a possession *that we who were the first to hope in Christ would be to the praise of His glory* (Ephesians 1:12).

Paul is still not finished praising the Lord for who He is and for what he has done. Thus far, we have learned about the Father who selected us and the Son who saved us.

We Need to Praise the Spirit Who Sealed Us

In Him, you also, after listening to the message of truth, the gospel of your salvation – having also believed, you were sealed in Him with the Holy Spirit of promise, who is given as a pledge of our inheritance, with a view to the redemption of God's own *possession, to the praise of His glory* (Ephesians 1:13-14).

We are sealed with the Holy Spirit of promise. The seal is an official stamp—a document that is put on us by God the Holy Spirit. To establish ownership, ranchers brand their cows with a red-hot branding iron. More significant, is the branding by the Holy Spirit in our hearts and lives that tells us we belong to Jesus Christ.

God has given us so much. We were chosen in the past, are accepted in the present, and will be secure in the future. Paul found it hard to stop writing because he was praising the Lord for all He had given him.

When a seal was put on a document after transaction, it meant the full price had been paid and ownership had been transferred. Our salvation is signed, sealed, and delivered!

3

Where We Are in Christ

The Book of Ephesians was written while Paul was in prison; yet when you open it, you do not smell the musty air of a prison. Instead, you feel the breezes of Calvary rise up and blow in your face as you open this powerful book. It is a book of victory; and if we want to be victorious, we must learn the truth that is delineated in Ephesians 1:15-17:

> *For this reason I too, having heard of the faith in the Lord Jesus which* exists *among you and your love for all the saints, do not cease giving thanks for you, while making mention* of *you in my prayers; that the God of our Lord Jesus Christ, the Father of glory, may give to you a spirit of wisdom and of revelation in the knowledge of Him.*

Paul was writing to an audience of awesome saints who were on their way to heaven and was praying for God to open their eyes and give them the spirit of wisdom and revelation in the knowledge of Him.

God designed us for dominion and mastery and to rule and reign.

We do not arrive in this life knowing everything we need to know. There is so much more to learn and apply to our lives.

I pray that *the eyes of your heart may be enlightened, so that you will know what is the hope of His calling, what are the riches of the glory of His inheritance in the saints and what is the surpassing greatness of His power toward us who believe.* These are *in accordance with the working of the strength of His might which He brought about in Christ, when He raised Him from the dead and seated Him at His right hand in the heavenly* places, *far above all rule and authority and power and dominion, and every name that is named, not only in this age but also in the one to come. And He put all things in subjection under His feet, and gave Him as head over all things to the church, which is His body, the fullness of Him who fills all in all* (Ephesians 1:18-23).

God designed us for dominion and mastery and to rule and reign; however, if we do not have dominion or mastery or are not ruling or reigning, then we are not living in the victory in which God designed us to live.

Then God said, "Let us make man in our image, after our likeness. And let them have dominion (Genesis 1:26 ESV). That is why God created us—to rule and have dominion. God did not make us to fail or be intimidated, stepped on, or misused. God gave man control over the earth and the ability to rule, and man was to be the master of the earth.

Let them have dominion over the fish of the sea and over the birds of the heavens and over the livestock and over all the earth and over every creeping thing that creeps on the earth (Genesis 1:26 ESV).

You make him to rule over the works of Your hands; You have put all things under his feet (Psalm 8:6).

When we watch the news, we recognize that man does not have dominion for we see and hear about death, disease, hate, war, crime, lust, sorrow, disappointment, and despair. It is obvious that man is not an overcomer but has been overcome. Rather than having dominion, he has been dominated. What has gone wrong?

The World Was Legally Lost

Man's dominion was lost by the first man.

And you were dead in your trespasses and sins (Ephesians 2:1).

How did we get to be *dead in trespasses and sins*? Paul explains:

And you were dead in your trespasses and sins, in which you formerly walked according to the course of this world, according to the prince of the power of the air, of the spirit that is now working in the sons of disobedience. Among them we too all formerly lived in the lusts of our flesh, indulging the desires of the flesh and of the mind, and were by nature children of wrath, even as the rest (Ephesians 2:1-3).

How did we get to be *children of wrath*? How did we get to be *sons of disobedience*? Where did we get this *nature*? Why is the devil called *the prince of the power of the air*? How did the devil become *the prince*?

Satan lost the war in heaven but gained a victory on earth.

I thought man was to have dominion. What happened? Satan rebelled against God and said, *I will make myself like the Most High* (Isaiah 14:14). However, no sooner had Satan unsheathed the sword of rebellion than the thunders of God's wrath rolled down the corridors of heaven and Satan was vanquished—kicked out of heaven. Because of this, Satan turned his attention to man.

Evil people have always known that if you cannot harm someone, harm someone that someone loves; and by doing so, you have harmed that someone anyway. Satan could not get to God so he tempted Adam and Eve to disobey—to achieve for themselves on earth what he himself had failed to do in heaven. Adam and Eve were tempted to become gods.

Satan had said he would make himself *like the Most High*, but it did not work in the heavens so he came down to earth and said to Adam and Eve, *Eat from it . . . and you will be like God* (Genesis 3:5). It was the same temptation. He tempted Adam and Eve to try to be on earth what he himself had failed to do and be in heaven.

Adam believed Satan's lie and gave in to the temptation to dethrone God and enthrone himself. However, Adam did not enthrone himself nor become God; instead, he became a servant. When Adam tried to dethrone God, he enthroned Satan who, though he failed to achieve a throne in heaven, now had a throne in the hearts and minds of man. Satan lost the war in heaven but gained a victory on earth.

The entire universe is ruled by divine law. What Adam lost in the Garden of Eden, he lost legally when he turned it over to Satan. The dominion and the authority that Adam had were legal gifts from God with no strings attached. Since it belonged to Adam, he could legally give it to someone else if he chose to. It was legally given and legally lost.

Furthermore, when Adam chose to obey Satan, he became Satan's slave. *Do you not know that when you present yourselves to someone as slaves for obedience, you are slaves of the one whom you obey, either of sin resulting in death, or of obedience resulting in righteousness?* (Romans 6:16).

When the devil tempted the Lord Jesus Christ, *the devil said to Him, "I will give You all this domain and its glory; for it has been handed over to me* (Luke 4:6). The power and the glory were delivered by Adam to the devil.

Jesus never disputed the devil's possessions. In fact, Jesus called the devil *the prince of this world* (John 14:30 NIV). Paul called the devil *the prince of the power of the air* (Ephesians 2:2 ESV) and *the god of this world* (2 Corinthians 4:4 ESV).

We need to understand this truth: The universe was lost legally. This is the main reason the Apostle Paul teaches that *our struggle is not against flesh and blood, but against the rulers, against the powers, against the world forces of this darkness, against the spiritual forces of wickedness in the heavenly places* (Ephesians 6:12).

The World Will Be Righteously Recovered

If dominion is to be regained, it must be legally regained. It was legally lost by the first Adam and will be righteously recovered by the second Adam. God's mighty plan in the universe, the battle of the ages, is that God is rightfully and legally going to reestablish and recover Adam's lost estate.

The dominion was given to a man, lost by a man, and will be legally recovered by a man.

Suppose God had just stopped and said, "Now, Adam, you gave it all to the devil; but since I'm God, I'm going to overlook your sin, take it all back from the devil by force, return it to you and then destroy the devil." If God had done that, God would not have been righteous. That would have made a farce of divine justice.

One thing is very clear: God owes the devil nothing; but if God is going to be true to His own righteousness and His own principles of justice, He must recover man's fallen estate and do it legally. Since it was legally given and legally lost, it must be legally recovered. If God did not do it legally, the devil would always be able to point a finger in the face of God and say, "You are not a God of justice or a God of righteousness."

Furthermore, man's dominion was lost by a man and, therefore, must be recovered by a man. It cannot be recovered by God acting as God alone. The dominion was given to a man, lost by a man, and will be legally recovered by a man. A member of Adam's race must be found upon whom

Satan has no claim in order to recover this dominion, but all of us are *by nature children of wrath* (Ephesians 2:3).

We are also the children of disobedience and walk according to the course of this world, according to the prince of the power of the air (Ephesians 2:2 KJV).

It must be legally reclaimed by a man, but that man cannot be a son of Adam for if he is a son of Adam, he is the son of a slave and all sons of slaves are slaves themselves.

God must find a man who can go and recover what Adam lost. He must be of Adam's race but a member over whom Satan has no legal claim. Since Adam was a slave, all of the sons of Adam are legally slaves; consequently, God has a problem. He must have a man, but that man cannot be a son of Adam. If he is not a man, it cannot be legally recovered; but if he is a son of Adam, he is already a slave and a slave cannot redeem a slave.

With all of this in mind, there had to be the incarnation of the Lord Jesus Christ and His virgin birth.

For since by a man came death, by a man also came the resurrection of the dead. For as in Adam all die, so also in Christ all will be made alive (1 Corinthians 15:21-22).

Therefore, since the children share in flesh and blood [the children of disobedience], He Himself likewise also partook of the same [Jesus came in flesh and blood], that through death He might render powerless him who had the power of death, that is, the devil (Hebrews 2:14).

What are these verses telling us? That Jesus became a man. The dominion was given to man legally, but man turned it over to the devil—legally given and legally lost. It must be legally reclaimed by a man, but that man cannot be a son of Adam for if he is a son of Adam, he is the son of a slave and all sons of slaves are slaves themselves. He must be a member of Adam's race without being a descendant of Adam. This is why Jesus Christ was conceived in the womb of Mary by the Holy Spirit.

Jesus did not overcome the devil with anything that is not available to us.

Satan came to Jesus in the wilderness with demonic temptation to try to get Jesus to sin and worship him. One instance of worship of Satan on Jesus' part and the whole plan of redemption would have collapsed. One sin on the part of Jesus would have given Satan the victory. Nevertheless, Satan knew he must seduce the last Adam as he did the first so he was aiming all the artillery of hell at the Son of God. *The devil took Him to a very high mountain and showed Him all the kingdoms of the world and their glory; and he said to Him, "All these things I will give You, if You fall down and worship me"* (Matthew 4:8-9). Had Jesus worshipped the devil, the devil knew he would not lose for he would have taken everything right back, and Jesus would have become a slave to Satan. But Jesus said to him, *Go, Satan! For it is written, "*YOU SHALL WORSHIP THE LORD YOUR GOD, AND SERVE HIM ONLY*"* (Luke 4:10).

The first Adam failed in a beautiful garden. The last Adam, the Lord Jesus Christ, overcame in a wilderness. Jesus did not challenge Satan's claim. I can imagine that

Jesus might have said, "Satan, I want you to know that I am God in human flesh. By the right and the prerogatives that are mine as God, I could speak a word and obliterate you right now. However, I am not going to overcome you as God; I am going to overcome you as a man."

Jesus Christ used the same two weapons that were available to Adam in the Garden of Eden and the same two weapons that are available to each of us.

1. **He used the Spirit of God:** *Jesus, full of the Holy Spirit, returned from the Jordan and was led around by the Spirit in the wilderness for forty days, being tempted by the devil* (Luke 4:1-2).
2. **He used the Word of God:** *Jesus answered him, "It is written, 'You shall worship the Lord your God and serve Him only'"* (Luke 4:8).

The same Holy Spirit that was available to Jesus Christ as a man is the same Holy Spirit that is available to us. The same Word of God that Jesus used as a man is the same Word of God that we have in our lives. Jesus did not overcome the devil with anything that is not available to us.

The devil later met Jesus in the Garden of Gethsemane where Jesus fought another battle. It appeared that Jesus would die of agony and a broken heart, but the Lord Jesus overcame the devil again. The final battle was bloody Calvary. The devil pushed Jesus to Calvary thinking that He would resist and rebel against the will of God. The hounds of hell were barking at the feet of Jesus Christ for His blood, yet Jesus willingly submitted His life to His Father. Perfectly innocent, Jesus bowed His head and died. He paid the full sin debt and recovered the lost estate for mankind. He bought back the redemption; He paid it in full.

But the battle was not over yet. Jesus Christ was in the grave; and the devil said, "Well, perhaps I can keep Him there. If I can keep Him in the grave, then I can win the victory."

Men of Israel, listen to these words: Jesus the Nazarene, a man attested to you by God with miracles and wonders and signs which God performed through Him in your midst, just as you yourselves know—this Man, *delivered over by the predetermined plan and foreknowledge of God, you nailed to a cross by the hands of godless men and put Him to death. But God raised* Him *up again, putting an end to the agony of death, since it was impossible for Him to be held in its power* (Acts 2:22-24).

The devil did the very best he could to hold the Lord Jesus in the grave. All the resources of the underworld were marshaled against Jesus, but He overcame death by the power of God. He was raised from the dead and later said, *I am He who lives, and was dead, and behold, I am alive forevermore. Amen. And I have the keys of Hades and of Death* (Revelation 1:18 NKJV). Jesus was victorious!

The World Will Be Gloriously Given

Born of a virgin, Jesus came to earth and lived a sinless life. He died—paying the ransom in full and buying back the lost estate. He paid with His own blood for *the wages of sin is death* (Romans 6:23). He was put in the grave; and though the devil tried to keep Him in the grave, He was raised by the power of God.

When Jesus Christ was raised from the dead, He *spoiled principalities and powers* (Colossians 2:15 KJV). The word *spoiled* means "to strip" as to strip the hide from an animal or "to disarm a defeated foe." When Jesus Christ came out of the grave, the kingdom of evil and darkness was thrown into complete bankruptcy and Satan's dominion had dissolved.

When Jesus Christ came out of the grave, the kingdom of evil and darkness was thrown into complete bankruptcy and Satan's dominion had dissolved.

Not only was it legally lost by a man and righteously recovered by a man and now available to every person on earth, but it has also been gloriously given.

> *But God, being rich in mercy, because of His great love with which He loved us, even when we were dead in our transgressions, made us alive together with Christ (by grace you have been saved), and raised us up with Him, and seated us with Him in the heavenly* places *in Christ Jesus* (Ephesians 2:4-6).

Jesus took our sins that we might be innocent and became guilty that we might be acquitted. He took our despair that we might be filled with joy and our shame that we might have His glory. He took the flames of hell that we might have the blessings of Heaven. His death and resurrection *made us alive together with Christ (by grace you have been saved)* (Ephesians 2:5).

WHEN HE ASCENDED ON HIGH, HE LED CAPTIVE A HOST OF CAPTIVES (Ephesians 4:8). Who was captive? The devil. The one who led us captive is now taken captive.

For we are members of His body, of His flesh and of His bones (Ephesians 5:30 KJV). We are a part of the Lord Jesus Christ. The Church is not merely an organization with

Jesus Christ as the President but a living entity with Jesus Christ as the head. If you are in Adam, all that belonged to Adam belongs to you. What belonged to Adam? Defeat, failure, and death. However, if you are in Christ, all that belongs to Christ belongs also to you for we are members of His body, of His Flesh, and of His bones.

Where is Jesus? He has ascended and was lifted far above all dominion and power. All things are beneath His feet.

> *That you will know what is the hope of His calling, what are the riches of the glory of His inheritance in the saints, what is the surpassing greatness of His power toward us who believe. These are in accordance with the working of the strength of His might which He brought about in Christ, when He raised Him from the dead and seated Him at His right hand in the heavenly places, far above all rule and authority and power and dominion, and every name that is named, not only in this age but also in the one to come. And He put all things in subjection under His feet* (Ephesians 1:18-22).

We are called to live life from a heavenly edge!

THE HEAVENLY BLESSINGS

4

Our Witness in Christ

We are called to be witnesses, not lawyers. A witness is someone who tells what they have seen and heard while a lawyer is someone who argues a case. We are witnesses of our Lord and Savior Jesus Christ.

A Christian with a glowing testimony is worth a library full of arguments. We need to learn how to give our testimony, and we do not have to be theologians in order to be able to do so.

When Jesus healed the man who was born blind, the Pharisees jumped the man's case because they were angry that Jesus had healed him. They backed him into a corner and began to ask him all kinds of theological questions. This man just said, *One thing I do know, that though I was blind, now I see* (John 9:25). A Christian with a testimony is never at the mercy of an infidel with an argument. Our testimony is the most convincing thing when we witness and share the Lord Jesus Christ.

> *And you were dead in your trespasses and sins in which you formerly walked according to the course of this world, according to the prince of the power of the air, of the spirit that is now working in the sons of disobedience. Among them we too all formerly lived in the lusts of our flesh, indulging the desires of the flesh and of the mind, and were by nature children of wrath, even as the rest. But God, being rich in mercy, because of His great love with which He loved us, even when we were dead in our transgressions, made us alive together with Christ (by grace you have been saved), and raised us up with Him, and seated us with Him in the heavenly places in Christ Jesus, so that in the ages to come He might show the surpassing riches of His grace in kindness toward us in Christ Jesus. For by grace you have been saved through faith; and that not of yourselves, it is the gift of God; not as a result of works, so that no one may boast. For we are His workmanship, created in Christ Jesus for good works, which God prepared beforehand so that we would walk in them* (Ephesians 2:1-10).

We are called to be witnesses to this fallen world. There are several tremendous truths regarding the testimony of a dead man.

We Should Reflect on Our Past Guilt

Christ made us alive when we were dead in our trespasses and sins. When people get saved, they need more than the forgiveness of sin; they need the forgiveness of sins. If you forgive a dead man, he is still dead. Death in the Bible is not the separation of the soul from the body but the separation of the soul from God. A man by nature is a man minus God.

When people get saved, they need more than the forgiveness of sin; they need the forgiveness of sins.

The Spirit of God inhabited Adam; but when Adam sinned because he ate of the forbidden fruit, God's Spirit departed from him for God had told him that if he disobeyed, he would die. However, the Bible also records that Adam went on to live for hundreds of years. God said he was going to die, and he did. He died immediately in the Spirit, progressively in his soul, and ultimately in his body. When **the Spirit of the Lord** departed from Adam, he was debased; when **the light** went out of Adam, he was darkened, and when **the life** went out of Adam, he was dead.

God describes every individual who is without Christ as being dead in trespasses and sin; and while having an existence, they have no life. Jesus said, *I came that they may have life* (John 10:10). Eternal life does not mean to exist in the natural world forever but to have Jesus.

Jesus raised three people from the dead:

1. **Jairus's daughter.** While the people laughed him to scorn, Jesus walked into the room of Jairus's little girl who had just died, took her by the hand, and told her to get up (Mark 5:35-43; Luke 8:49-56).
2. **The widow's son.** A young man was being carried out of the city of Nain for burial when Jesus had compassion on the mother, interrupted the funeral

processional, and raised the widow's son from the dead (Luke 7:11-17).
3. **Lazarus.** He had been buried for four days, and decay and the stench of death had already set in. Jesus told them to roll away the stone, and He raised Lazarus from the dead (John 11:1-46).

Those who are without the Lord Jesus Christ are the walking dead of this world and are living under the dictatorship of the devil while talking about how free they are.

We often look at young boys and girls and express how sweet they are. If we are not careful, we will conclude that they are not dead in their trespasses and sin. We know a thief, a pervert, a liar, an adulterer, and a drunkard are all dead in their sins. At the same time, boys and girls in our churches who are at the age of accountability but do not know Jesus are just as dead in their sins and trespasses as the worst bank robber or drunkard on skid row. Whether it is a little girl in her bedroom or Lazarus in a grave, we are **dead** in trespasses and sin.

There was a time when we were devilish and *formerly walked according to the course of this world, according to the prince of the power of the air, of the spirit that is now working in the sons of disobedience* (Ephesians 2:2).

Those who are without the Lord Jesus Christ are the walking dead of this world and are living under the dictatorship of the devil while talking about how free they are. However, they are not free at all but are slaves. They are free to do what they want but not free to do what they ought. They are not free to live until they have the power of Jesus in their lives. Jesus came *that they may have life, and have it abundantly* (John 10:10); yet people without Christ are not only dead but also devilish and disobedient.

Those who are without the Lord Jesus Christ are the walking dead of this world. They are not free to live until they have the power of Jesus in their lives.

The Apostle Paul talks about *the spirit that is now working in the sons of disobedience* (Ephesians 2:2). Mankind is inherently disobedient and rebellious. A child does not have to be taught to lie or steal; a child must be taught NOT to lie or steal. Children are dead in their sins, devilish, and disobedient.

Among them we too all formerly lived in the lusts of our flesh, indulging the desires of the flesh and of the mind, and were by nature children of wrath, even as the rest (Ephesians 2:3). We are all sinners, born with a depraved nature. David said, *In sin my mother conceived me* (Psalm 51:5). Before we even began school, we already knew how to lie and deceive.

As I have traveled throughout the nations of the world, I have made it a priority to visit hundreds of cemeteries in various towns and cities. Every time I visit a cemetery, I am reminded of the brevity of life and the solemn statistic that one out of one dies.

The Apostle Paul stated that *you were dead in your trespasses and sins* (Ephesians 2:1), yet Christ has conquered sin and destroyed death. When I stood in front of the grave of Charles Haddon Spurgeon, I was reminded of what he said in a sermon: "The day will come when you will hear that Charles Haddon Spurgeon has died. On that day, do not believe a word of it. I will be more alive than I have ever been before!"

We Need to Recall Our Present Grace

But God, being rich in mercy, because of His great love with which He loved us, even when we were dead in our transgressions, made us alive together with Christ (by grace you have been saved) (Ephesians 2:4-5).

While we were dead in sin, Christ saved us. **He restored us**, gave us life, and quickened us together in Him. Quickened means to revive, restore, and give life. This is the reason that salvation must be by grace. A dead person cannot bring themselves back to life. Jairus's daughter had no power to bring herself back to life nor did the widow's son or Lazarus. If God did not take the initiative, none of us would be saved. The Lord took the initiative to raise the dead physically and has taken the initiative to raise us spiritually. Most people do not understand that it takes a miracle for a person to be saved. How would you attempt to raise a dead man?

1. You could give him an **example** of how a dead man ought to live by doing deep knee bends and push-ups and walking around to see if this would have an impact. Obviously, this would not work; yet most people think that Jesus came as an example. Salvation does not come by learning lessons from the life of Christ but by receiving life from the death of Christ. It is impossible to raise a dead man by example.
2. You could place the dead man in a powerful **environment**. Put him in a room full of people and see if it brings him to life. This is the way some try to deal with the sin problem. The Garden of Eden was the best environment this world has ever known, but Adam and Eve still fell into sin.

3. You could try a lot of **encouragement**. You could encourage him to get up and come alive again by saying, "You have it in you! Open your eyes! Stretch!" A lot of church services are simply pep rallies because they think they just must encourage one another to do better and to live better. People come down the aisles of churches and clasp the hands of pastors and say, "I'm going to do better, Pastor, because you have really encouraged me today." Encouragement will not make a dead man live.
4. You could try **education**. Give him *The Ten Lessons on Life* and say, "Read this book." There is futility in all of this because it takes a miracle to raise a dead man. Our salvation is as big a miracle as the resurrection when Christ got up and walked out of the grave.

What Is This Grace?

We were **restored** and then we were **raised** for He *raised us up with Him, and seated us with Him in the heavenly places in Christ Jesus* (Ephesians 2:6). When our Lord saves us and gives us life, He does not leave us in the grave. When Lazarus was in the grave, Jesus spoke to him and said, *Lazarus, come forth* (John 11:43). He meant for Lazarus not only to have life but also to have liberty—to get out of that grave and be raised up.

Our Lord gives us power to live the Christian life. Our testimony tells everyone that Christ saved us and gave us the power to live a victorious Christian life. He broke the power of canceled sin and set the prisoner free. God gives strength and power day by day. Thank God for the grace of the Lord Jesus Christ who not only has restored us but also *raised us up with Him, and seated us with Him in the heavenly places in Christ Jesus* (Ephesians 2:6).

What a difference between those who do not understand the grace of God and those who do. Those who do not work feverishly trying to earn a piece of real estate in heaven, but we do not have to wait to die to go to heaven for we are now seated in the heavenlies. The heavenlies is not a place we visit from time to time but is to be our permanent dwelling place.

The Lord Jesus Christ is now resting in His finished work; consequently, I am also resting with Him in His finished work.

There is little difference between heaven and the heavenlies. The heavenlies is the sphere of victory where every Christian lives day by day. The Lord Jesus has been raised up and is sitting on the right hand of the Father in the heavenlies. When Jesus died, we died with Him; when He came out of the grave, we came out with Him spiritually; and when He was seated, we were seated with Him. The Lord Jesus Christ is now resting in His finished work; consequently, I am also resting with Him in His finished work.

We tell people many times to keep looking up when we are already up. All things are beneath us, and we are seated with the Lord Jesus in the heavenlies. There is only one way you can look, and that is down. We cannot get any higher than to be raised with the Lord Jesus Christ. We have been restored, raised, and then rested!

Alfred Hitchcock was a phenomenal storyteller and movie producer. In 1964, he produced the movie, *The*

Coffin Maker, a story about a young man who committed many acts of terrible violence and was placed in prison.

In this prison was a man who had the responsibility of making coffins. The young man who had committed many acts of violence became good friends with the coffin maker; and between them, they devised a sinister plan to get the young man out of prison. They decided that when the next person in the prison died, the coffin maker would make a coffin for him. Then the young man would sneak into the area where the coffin was located, get inside, and lie next to the deceased.

After some time had passed, another convict died in prison; and a coffin was quickly made for him. The young man snuck into the area where the coffin was located, looking carefully to make sure no one had seen him. Then he hurriedly lifted the lid of the coffin and lay down next to the deceased, pulling the coffin lid quickly back in place.

He suddenly heard muffled voices but was unable to understand what they were saying. He felt the coffin being lifted and began to think it would not be much longer before he would be free. He felt the coffin being taken down the stairs and heard the metal doors of the prison rattle when they were opened. The young man smiled while lying next to the deceased thinking, "I am on my way home today. It will not be much longer before I am free."

The backdoor of the hearse was opened and the coffin pushed inside. He felt the jolt when the coffin hit the back wall of the hearse. When he heard the engine start, he knew he was headed to the nearby cemetery which was filled with old gravestones and was in a terrible run-down condition.

The prison hearse was driven to the nearby cemetery; and when the backdoor was opened, the convict in the coffin could hear muffled voices again. Suddenly, the coffin was pulled out of the hearse and carried to the place of burial. Once the coffin arrived, it was lowered into the hole in the ground. When the coffin hit the bottom of the hole, the young man said to himself, "If they bury me, my friend the coffin maker will dig me up. I am headed home today!"

If you could be saved by good works, then you could boast about it. If you are saved by God's grace, then you must give God all of the glory.

Clots of dirt landed loudly on the lid of the casket as the coffin was covered with dirt and the hole was filled. The young man in the coffin began to cry loudly, "Hurry! Dig me up!" A few moments later, he began to feel the coolness of the earth creeping into the coffin. In desperation, he reached into his shirt pocket and pulled out a lighter. When he flicked on the lighter, he saw the face of the coffin maker and realized he had gone to the grave with the wrong person.

If we go to the grave with the wrong person, we will not be able to get out of the grave. If we go to the grave with Christ in our hearts, we will experience resurrection! But for God's grace and the miracle of salvation, we were dead, debased, and darkened; however, Christ raised us up into heavenly places to rest in Him.

The last testimony aspect of a dead man is that:

We Need to Realize Our Prospective Glory

God does this *so that in the ages to come He might show the surpassing riches of His grace in kindness toward us in Christ*

Jesus. For by grace you have been saved through faith; and that not of yourselves, it is the gift of God; not as a result of works, so that no one may boast. For we are His workmanship, created in Christ Jesus for good works, which God prepared beforehand so that we would walk in them (Ephesians 2:7-10).

Paul writes about the ages to come and explains the Lord's purpose for us in eternity where we are going to be part of a great, great exhibition that God has saved by His grace and to whom He might show the exceeding riches of His grace.

God's purpose and God's plan are linked together, and God's plan coincides with God's purpose to *show the surpassing riches of His grace* (Ephesians 2:7). *For by grace you have been saved through faith; and that not of yourselves, it is the gift of God; not as a result of works, so that no one may boast* (Ephesians 2:8-9).

God will not share His glory with another. If you could be saved by good works, then you could boast about it. If you are saved by God's grace, then you must give God all of the glory. If you are saved by grace, then works do not have anything to do with it. If you are suspended by a chain of ten thousand links and one of those links is made of crepe paper, how safe are you? If one link in the chain of salvation depends upon you, you will never make it for God is in the business of receiving the glory.

God is not keeping score because we are not saved by the merit of man but by the mercy of God and not by the goodness of man but by the grace of God. This grace is not only **saving grace**, but it is also **sanctifying grace**. Some get the idea that because we are saved by grace, it does not make any difference how we live.

For we are His workmanship, created in Christ Jesus for good works (Ephesians 2:10). We have saving grace, sanctifying grace, and **surviving grace**.

God's grace never turns loose of us. I believe in eternal security because we get it by grace, and the grace that saves us is the grace that also keeps us. If we get it by works, then when our works fail, we lose it.

We have saving grace, sanctifying grace, surviving grace, and **sure grace**. We have confidence in the grace of God. We know that we are saved and sitting in the heavenlies.

God's purpose and God's plan result in God's praise.

We are saved by grace through faith. It is grace that saves us, and faith simply reaches up and takes hold of God's grace saying, "I believe it, and I want to be saved." When God's hand of grace meets your hand of faith, that is salvation!

However, even the faith we have is a gift of God for out of our debased, devilish, disobedient, dead hearts, we do not possess the faith to save us. God puts faith in our hearts, and that is the only reason anyone can be saved.

> *For by grace you have been saved through faith; and that not of yourselves, it is the gift of God; not as a result of works, so that no one may boast. For we are His workmanship, created in Christ Jesus for good works, which God prepared beforehand so that we would walk in them* (Ephesians 2:8-10).

Why did God save me? What was God's plan? What was God's grace? *For we are His workmanship, created in Christ Jesus for good works, which God prepared beforehand so that we would walk in them* (Ephesians 2:10). Why do we do good works? Not in order to be saved but because we have been saved. We are not saved by works but by faith that works.

God's purpose and God's plan result in God's praise. The summation of our spiritual biography:

- What we were — past guilt
- What we are — present grace
- What we shall be — prospective glory

This is what makes Christianity different from any other religion. Thank God for His grace!

Our Worship in Christ

There is a familiar saying that God never does anything apart from the prayers of His people. Accurate or not, I do believe we usually underestimate the power of prayer and overemphasize the power of our own performance. God desires that we learn how to pray effectively for one another. As we pray, our prayers rise to heaven; and our desire is that these prayers will leave an impact on earth.

> *To me, the very least of all saints, this grace was given, to preach to the Gentiles the unfathomable riches of Christ, and to bring to light what is the administration of the mystery which for ages has been hidden in God who created all things; so that the manifold wisdom of God might now be made known through the church to the rulers and the authorities in the heavenly* places. *This was in accordance with the eternal purpose which*

He carried out in Christ Jesus our Lord, in whom we have boldness and confident access through faith in Him. Therefore I ask you not to lose heart at my tribulations on your behalf, for they are your glory. For this reason I bow my knees before the Father (Ephesians 3:8-14).

Paul wrote this letter while he was in prison as he had a burden on his heart to pray for the church in Ephesus. His spirit was soaring out of that prison!

We usually underestimate the power of prayer and overemphasize the power of our own performance.

In reality, stone walls do not make a prison nor iron bars a cage. You cannot imprison someone who knows how to pray. Even though there are believers who are not able to attend church due to illness, they can touch the heart of God and move mountains if they know how to pray. Just the thought of Paul on his knees in prison ought to inspire us to learn how to pray in such a manner as to shake the heavenlies. While most of us would have been praying, "God, please get me out of this prison!" Paul was interceding that the Church glow up, grow down, and go out!

For this reason I bow my knees before the Father, from whom every family in heaven and on earth derives its name, that He would grant you, according to the riches of His glory, to be strengthened with power through His Spirit in the inner man, so that Christ may dwell in your hearts through faith; and that you, being rooted and grounded in love, may be able to comprehend with all the saints what is the breadth and length and height and depth, and to know the love of Christ which surpasses knowledge, that you may be filled up to all the fullness of God (Ephesians 3:14-19).

What follows next is the confidence displayed in the prayer as he brings it to a close: *Now to Him who is able to do far more abundantly beyond all that we ask or think, according to the power that works within us, to Him be the glory in the church and in Christ Jesus to all generations* (Ephesians 3:20-21).

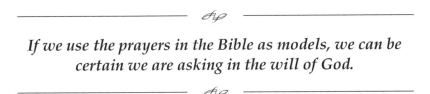

If we use the prayers in the Bible as models, we can be certain we are asking in the will of God.

We must learn to intercede for our children, spouses, pastors, neighbors, and friends; but most of us wonder what we should pray about and how we should pray because there are so many needs and problems. There are times we need to pray specifically concerning a mate, a college, a career path, or a health issue; and if we use the prayers in the Bible as models and begin to ask for our loved ones like the Apostle Paul asked for those he loved, we can be certain we are asking in the will of God. We can then pray with great faith and confidence before the Lord. It will open a whole new world of prayer and praying with power.

There are many reasons to pray for another and in such a manner that will produce powerful results.

Spiritual Wealth for Their Needfulness

We are to pray for people to have spiritual wealth for their needfulness—not monetary wealth.

To me, the very least of all saints, this grace was given, to preach to the Gentiles the unfathomable riches of Christ, and to bring to light what is the administration of the mystery which for ages has been hidden in God who created all things; so that the manifold wisdom of God might now be made known through the church to the rulers and the authorities in the heavenly places. This was in accordance with the eternal purpose which He carried out in Christ Jesus our Lord, in whom we have boldness and confident access through faith in Him. Therefore I ask you not to lose heart at my tribulations on your behalf, for they are your glory. For this reason I bow my knees before the Father (Ephesians 3:8-14).

Paul wanted the people in Ephesus to know how rich they were. Though they had needs, he asked God to help them understand the unsearchable riches of Christ Jesus and know the eternal purpose of God.

Many believers go to church three times a week, sing in the choir, give their tithe and offerings yet their children are out dabbling in the world because they do not know how rich they are in Christ.

Moses refused to be called the son of Pharaoh's daughter because he esteemed the riches of God a greater treasure than all the treasures of Egypt. We will not be sucked into Egypt when we understand what we have in the Lord Jesus Christ.

If you have had a wonderful meal and are then offered a plate full of stale crumbs, you would say, "No, thank you. I'm already satisfied." When you have been feasting on the Lord Jesus Christ and understand who He is and all He has done for you, you do not have to be out in the back alley eating out of trash cans because you can say, "I am satisfied in the Lord Jesus Christ."

Most of us are far too interested in our children becoming wealthy, healthy, and happy rather than their becoming holy.

Many young people have never found their true satisfaction in Jesus. Though they may be saved, they do not understand the riches they have in Christ—God's wealth and God's riches for their needfulness. We need to pray that the Lord will open their eyes and hearts to see and know how rich they are in Christ. A lot of people are going to heaven, but they are going second class. When I say second class, I am not talking about physical or monetary wealth or the lack thereof.

Most of us are far too interested in our children becoming wealthy, healthy, and happy rather than their becoming holy. We are often far more interested in early retirement in order to enjoy personal wealth instead of our eternal wealth in Christ. We are more excited about financial bonuses from our employer than with the divine reality of our eternal treasures.

The Lord wants us to become strong in our spirits and be filled with the Holy Spirit! As we learn how to pray for others, we need to be able to pray for God's provision for their needfulness.

Spiritual Strength for Their Weakness

The average prayer meeting usually goes something like, "Lord, bless Suzy who's sick. God, bless John who's ill. God, encourage Richard who's not doing well." There is nothing wrong with praying for the sick, but we seem to be so focused on the health of our children, friends, and ourselves that the prayer meeting turns into an "organ recital." It is all about livers, lungs, hearts, and spleens.

God never has any overdrafts.

What we need to hear parents say is, "Pray for my son, pray for my daughter, that they would be mighty in the Spirit." That is what Paul prayed. He did not ask for health or wealth for them but that they would see the true riches of Christ Jesus and be strengthened with might in their inner beings. God will do that according to the riches of His glory. God never has any overdrafts. He is sufficient to strengthen them in their inner beings, but the Bible does not say it is out of His riches. A rich man might give you $5 out of his riches, but that may not be according to his riches. However, God wants to bless according to His riches.

Some think that being Spirit-filled is for adults but not for children, but that is not true *for the promise is for you and your children and for all who are far off, as many as the Lord our God will call to Himself.* (Acts 2:39). We need to teach our children to walk in the Spirit and to be filled with the Spirit.

Early on Sunday morning, September 2, 1945, aboard the new 45,000-ton battleship USS Missouri and before representatives of nine Allied Nations, the Japanese surrendered. At the ceremony, General MacArthur stated that the Japanese and their conquerors did not meet "in a spirit of mistrust, malice or hatred but rather, it is for us, both victors and vanquished, to rise to that higher dignity which alone benefits the sacred purposes we are about to serve."

The USS Missouri has been described as the most famous battleship ever built. Before finally being decommissioned in 1992, the Mighty Mo received three battle stars for its service in World War II and five for the Korean War as well as two Combat Action Ribbons and several commendations and medals for the Gulf War.

In total, the USS Missouri, "Big Mo" and "Mighty Mo," earned 11 Battle Stars for her service in World War II, the Korean War, and the Gulf War. She was one of the most decorated US Navy ships in history, having earned over 15 ribbons.

Even though Mighty Mo had sailed the seven seas and fought historic battles, she got stuck in the mud on one occasion while sailing out of the Chesapeake Bay area. Even though no one was hurt, the battleship remained stuck for two weeks. After a period of time, the tide came in deep enough to lift the ship and set her free.

Though we are often spiritually victorious in our lives, there are times that we get stuck just like Mighty Mo. We must keep praising and praying as the water of the Spirit is still flowing. We will be lifted up when the spiritual tide flows in.

Spiritual Depth for Their Shallowness

So that Christ may dwell in your hearts through faith; and that you, being rooted and grounded in love, may be able to comprehend with all the saints what is the breadth and length and height and depth, and to know the love of Christ which surpasses knowledge (Ephesians 3:17-19).

Paul did not want them to be shallow Christians but to be rooted and solid so that Christ might dwell in their hearts by faith. Dwell is a domestic term that means to be at home, to settle down, to be welcome.

Rooted is a horticultural term. Paul wanted their roots to go deep. The root is the part of the tree that only God sees. Sometimes as we watch our young people go off to college and get involved in drugs and sexual immorality, we wonder what went wrong. They were not rooted.

Grounded is an architectural term. We are to have a foundation on which to stand.

During my teenage years, my father launched a family business called Davis Brothers Nursery and Grandma's Garden Shop. We grew more than 30,000 hanging baskets along with tens of thousands of shrubberies.

I learned so much about life and leadership during my teenage years because with our family business came the responsibility of designing and constructing the greenhouses across our acreage. When building strong greenhouses, it is critical to dig deep post holes. It takes a lot of hard, tenacious work to build a strong foundation. Once all of the post holes are dug and the 4x4 posts placed and secured in the holes, the roof can be solidly placed and secured on the posts, and the greenhouse built. The key is that the foundation must be strong.

Consequently, we pray for spiritual wealth for their needfulness, spiritual strength for their weakness, and spiritual depth for their shallowness. We want them to be grounded and rooted for the tests of life that will come.

Some people think the church is on its way out, but that is not scriptural. Jesus called the church out, sent the church out, and will soon return to take the church out. The greatest organization on the face of the earth is a Spirit-filled, New Testament, Bible-believing, Christ-honoring, worshipping, praising Church.

The greatest organization on the face of the earth is a Spirit-filled, New Testament, Bible-believing, Christ-honoring, worshipping, praising Church.

The global Church is growing faster today than it ever has in human history, and the Church is not on its way out in the sense that the world thinks. The devil does not like what is happening, and we are in a great spiritual struggle as we see colossal forces colliding. It is not the time to be sleeping.

Dr. James Dobson, founder of Focus on the Family, once shared a story concerning a missionary in a remote jungle. One day the missionary opened the door to his hut and found a gigantic snake inside—something like a boa constrictor or a python. The snake was so large it could swallow a pig whole.

The missionary went out to his car and got his revolver. When he checked his gun for bullets, he found only one in the chamber. The missionary went back inside the hut and carefully aimed at the head of that monstrous snake, pulled the trigger, and hit the snake directly in the head. Even though the snake was mortally wounded, it did not die right away but began to writhe and thrash about with its body going this way and that. The snake literally tore up everything in the hut as it was dying.

At Calvary, Jesus put a bullet directly into Satan's head. What we are now seeing are the death throes of one who has been mortally wounded by the cross of Christ.

We are in a battle, and the serpent is twisting and writhing and wreaking havoc, but we have already won the victory in Christ Jesus!

Spiritual Perspective for Their Narrowness

> *That you, being rooted and grounded in love, may be able to comprehend with all the saints what is the breadth and length and height and depth, and to know the love of Christ which surpasses knowledge* (Ephesians 3:17-19).

Be broadminded enough to love the different streams of Christianity that make up the Church.

Paul is teaching us not to be narrow minded, when he mentions all the saints and knowing the love of Christ. We should pray that we and our children will love the people of God, love the Church, and be broadminded enough to love the different streams of Christianity that make up the Church.

God is going to bless some people we do not think He ought to bless. There are those who are a part of different streams of Christianity who do not walk and talk like we do; however, they are part of the family of God. We should seek to have a current Christian worldview.

As Christians, we must love the entire body of Christ, not just our own tribe. There are those who actually believe that their tribe alone will complete the Great Commission and be the only ones who will go to heaven.

We need to become global Christians and love the people of God and pray for all the saints, not just "our saints." Consider praying on:

- Monday for Mexico and the Caribbean
- Tuesday for Central America
- Wednesday for Africa
- Thursday for Europe
- Friday for the Middle East
- Saturday for the Far East
- Sunday for North America

When self is on the throne, Christ is on the cross; and when Christ is on the throne, self is on the cross.

With all the saints what is the breadth and length and height and depth (Ephesians 3:18). Imagine the dimensions of the cross. Look at Jesus' right nail-pierced hand and think of the breadth of God's love. Look at His left nail-pierced hand and think of the length of God's love. Look at His thorn-crowned brow and think of the height of God's love. Look at His nail-pierced feet and think of the depth of God's love. This is the full love of God! We will never be motivated to fulfill the Great Commission together until we truly love all the tribes of Christianity.

Do we view our lives as a river or a reservoir? Do we see ourselves as a container or a channel? Do we have a small pie mentally, or do we believe there is no limit to God's resources?

The story is told about a man whose car broke down in the Mojave Desert. He got out of the car and began walking through the hot desert to try to find help. Eventually, he began to climb a small hill but did not have the strength to get to the top and collapsed and died. Just on the other side of the hill was an oasis with fruit trees where he would have been able to sustain life until help arrived. He almost made it, but almost was not good enough.

Some have begun this powerful journey only to fail to reach maturity; however, we must continue to strive to reach our maximum potential as Christians. *That you may be filled up to all the fullness of God* (Ephesians 3:19). The Lord has not called us to be empty but to experience His fullness every day.

Spiritual Fullness for Their Emptiness

We are going to have trouble when we are empty, when we are not full of Jesus. When someone jostles us, whatever we are full of is going to spill out. We are either going to be full of Jesus or full of self. When self is on the throne, Christ is on the cross; and when Christ is on the throne, self is on the cross. Paul is praying that we *may be filled up to all the fullness of God.*

We are a blessing when we are overflowing. There is nothing more pathetic than to see a half-empty Christian trying to overflow. However, when we are filled with *all the fullness of God,* we will bless people even when we do not even know we are blessing them. Sometimes people come up to me and express that I have been a blessing to them. I did not know I was blessing them by what I said or did; I had no idea. We should pray that our fullness overflows on our family, friends, and colleagues.

These five powerful prayer principles are in sync with the will of God and inspire us to pray. *This is the confidence which we have before Him, that, if we ask anything according to His will, He hears us* (1 John 5:14).

Sometimes we pray but do not know if we are praying in the will of God. We express words like, "I hope this is the will of God," or "I hope you get that new job or that great scholarship." At other times, we ask God for things

He does not want us to have. In all of these instances, Paul's prayer is the prayer God will answer: *Now to Him who is able to do far more abundantly beyond all that we ask or think, according to the power that works within us* (Ephesians 3:20).

If we feel or sense our prayer was not answered, it is not because our prayer exceeded God's power but because God's plan exceeded our prayer.

We need to have our minds on God's power when we pray, not on the problems. If we feel or sense our prayer was not answered, it is not because our prayer exceeded God's power but because God's plan exceeded our prayer.

Paul also says, *In the same way the Spirit also helps our weakness; for we do not know how to pray as we should, but the Spirit Himself intercedes for* us *with groanings too deep for words* (Romans 8:26). We should glance at our problems and gaze at God's power.

We should not only **keep God's power in mind** but also **God's praise**. *To Him be the glory in the church and in Christ Jesus to all generations forever and ever. Amen* (Ephesians 3:21).

When our prayers are for the glory of God, we will see things begin to happen. Unto Him be glory in the Church! Look at your prayers in light of God's power and God's praise. If we are having difficulty with prayer, we should praise Him and we will have an ocean to swim in. *To Him be the glory in the church and in Christ Jesus to all generations forever and ever. Amen.* The next time you pray for a loved one, a friend, a colleague, or an acquaintance, just lay it out there and begin to pray these five powerful prayers for them. You will wrestle and win!

THE HONORABLE BEHAVIOR

Our Wholeness in Christ

A man was shipwrecked on a deserted island and had to learn to feed and take care of himself until many years later when someone came to rescue him.

He had taken care of things pretty well and had built a nice house. Next to the house, he had constructed a church and had even put a steeple on top. Next to the church was another fine, magnificent building.

Those who rescued him asked what the buildings were. He responded, "Well, that's my house where I live." They then queried, "What is next door? It looks like a church." He said, "It is a church. I built myself a church." They asked, "Well, what is that other building for then?" "Oh," he said, "that's another church. I had an argument in the old one and moved to another church." Many of our problems often come from within.

Paul implored us to be *diligent to preserve the unity of the Spirit in the bond of peace* (Ephesians 4:3), and the Book of Psalms tells us *Behold, how good and how pleasant it is for brothers to dwell together in unity!* (133:1). Proverbs 6 enumerates seven things God hates, the seventh being *one who spreads strife among brothers* (v.19).

**We must never let anyone tell us
that doctrine does not matter.**

This is a God-given harmony called the unity of the Spirit. We cannot produce it; however, we strive to preserve it. This harmony is based on several basic concepts.

The Ground of Our Harmony Is Truth

It is doctrinal and spiritual: *Being diligent to preserve the unity of the Spirit in the bond of peace. There is one body and one Spirit, just as also you were called in one hope of your calling; one Lord, one faith, one baptism, one God and Father of all who is over all and through all and in all* (Ephesians 4:3-6).

We must never let anyone tell us that doctrine does not matter. If the Church ceases to hold these great truths, she will lose her unity. However, unity does not mean unison. Being in unison may be acceptable for those in a choir; but everyone does not have to sing the same note. We can sing in harmony without singing in unison.

Neither am I talking about uniformity. We do not have to be a church of clones where everyone must look and dress alike. It is not that we are serving with uniformity for uniformity comes from without while unity comes from within.

Unison and unity are not necessarily the same. We can be in the same church and yet not be in unity. If you take two tom cats, tie their tails together, and hang them over a clothesline, you have union but NOT unity!

There are seven truths that make up our unity:

1. One body. *Unity of the Spirit* (Ephesians 4:3). That one body is the Church of our Lord and Savior Jesus Christ—a spiritual body. The Church is not a corporation with Jesus as the president; the Church is a body with Jesus as the head. That makes all the difference in the world.

There is a local expression of that body. There is the great universal Church which is made up of local New Testament bodies. When anyone sows discord in the church, they dishonor the head who is Jesus and wound themselves because we are members of the same body.

2. One Spirit. *There is one body and one Spirit, just as also you were called in one hope of your calling* (Ephesians 4:4). Paul is talking about the Holy Spirit who is the substance of our life, the secret of our strength, the source of our unity, and the one who binds us together and tells us that we belong to one another.

Not only does God's Spirit bear witness with our spirit that we are children of God, but God's Spirit also bears witness with our spirit that we belong to one another. Dr. Vance Havner said: "We're not to be wired together by organization, frozen together by formalism, rusted together by tradition, but melted together by one Spirit."

As we strive to network instead of not-work, we should strive to bring harmony throughout the body of Christ. We do not have the same skills, but we can have the same goal: that everyone has access to the gospel.

3. One Hope. *There is one body and one Spirit, just as also you were called in one hope of your calling* (Ephesians 4:4). That one hope is the Second Coming of Jesus Christ—the Blessed Hope. All true believers in Christ are waiting for Jesus Christ to come again.

All true believers in Christ are waiting for Jesus Christ to come again.

We may have different views of the Second Coming of Jesus, such as amillennial, pre-millennial and post-millennial. The longer I serve Christ, the more I simply want to say, *Even so, come, Lord Jesus* (Revelation 22:20 KJV). I believe we are getting very close to His return.

The more I survey what is going on in our world today, the more I am convinced that Jesus is coming soon! He spoke of the signs of the end-time—*great earthquakes shall be in diverse places, and famines, and pestilences; and fearful sights and great signs shall there be from heaven* (Luke 21:11 KJV). Then Jesus said, "*All these are the beginning of sorrows*" (Matthew 24:8 KJV).

The word for "sorrows" is the same as the word for "birth pains." When a woman is going to deliver a baby, she has what is called sorrows.

Jesus said, *But when these things begin to take place, straighten up and lift up your heads, because your redemption is drawing near* (Luke 21:28). Without meaning to be a sensationalist, I sincerely believe we are living in the closing shadows of an age; and our one hope—the only hope—of this world is the Second Coming of our Lord and Savior Jesus Christ.

As the Church races toward the finish line for the completion of the Great Commission, there is a prophetic aspect of speeding up the return of Christ. May we be renewed in our Blessed Hope!

On October 12, 2019, Eliud Kipchoge of Kenya, age 34, achieved a milestone once believed to be unattainable. On a misty Saturday morning in Vienna, Austria, in an athletic spectacle of historic proportions on a course specially chosen for speed, he ran 26.2 miles in a once-inconceivable time of 1 hour 59 minutes 40 seconds.

In becoming the first person to cover the marathon distance in less than two hours, Kipchoge achieved a sports milestone, granting him almost mythical status in the running world by breaking through a barrier that many would have deemed untouchable only a few years before.

Kipchoge, an eight-time major marathon winner and three-time Olympic medalist, pounded his chest twice as he crossed the finish line in Vienna's leafy Prater Park where the majority of the run had unfolded on a long straightaway of recently paved road with roundabouts on either end.

For Kipchoge, the feat merely burnished his credentials as the world's greatest marathoner. "Together, when we run, we can make this world a beautiful world," Kipchoge said after finishing.

Along Kipchoge's journey, there had to have been more times than we will ever know when he did not want to practice and, no doubt, numerous times during a race when he wanted to quit. However, he was never a "no show" on race day! What he began, he saw to the finish. His final words, "Together, when we run, we can make this world a beautiful world," challenge us to run our Christian race to the finish line.

There will be times when we do not want to show up for our practice sessions in prayer and Bible study. While we are running to overcome life's challenges, there will be instances when we will wonder if it is all worth it or we will feel like giving up, giving in, and giving over to the temptations of the world. But if we run together, we can do more than make this world a "beautiful world"; we can help to make it a saved world.

There will be times when we do not want to show up for our practice sessions in prayer and Bible study.

---

4. One Lord. Paul mentions *one Lord* in Ephesians 4:5. Jesus Christ is that one Lord. The early church did not call him Jesus nearly as frequently as they called Him Lord. Perhaps we need to get in the habit of calling Him "Lord Jesus."

Jesus did not come to take sides—not one organization over another nor one church over another nor one person over another.

When Joshua came against the pagan city of Jericho, he went out to consider the situation and became aware of a presence behind him. When he wheeled around, he saw a man with a drawn sword. Joshua was astounded and said, *Are you for us or for our adversaries?* (Joshua 5:13). The man with the drawn sword said, *No; rather I indeed come now as captain of the host of the* L<small>ORD</small> (Joshua 5:14). In essence he was saying, "Look, I'm not for them, and I'm not for you. I haven't come to take sides. I've come to take over."

The one Lord, the captain of the Lord's host, is Jesus Christ Himself who is the head of the Church. Jesus must always be the Lord of the Church.

5. One Faith. Paul mentions *one faith* in Ephesians 4:5. The one faith he is talking about is the unified body of truth that we call the Bible. Not faith, not a faith, but one faith. Jude talked about the same thing: *Beloved, while I was making every effort to write you about our common salvation, I felt the necessity to write to you appealing that you contend earnestly for the faith which was once for all handed down to the saints* (v.3). There is one faith—God's revealed Word, and we are to earnestly contend for it.

We need to get a bulldog grip on the Bible and never let go for there is only one faith. We do not need a new and modern gospel for a new and a modern age. If it is new, it is not true. If it is not absolute, it is obsolete. It is the one faith for our church and for **the** Church. We can have all other kinds of programs, but we must have this one faith.

Just before he stepped off the scene, the Apostle Paul said: *I have fought the good fight, I have finished the course, I have kept the faith* (2 Timothy 4:7). He was faithful to the fight, faithful to the finish, and faithful to the faith!

6. One Baptism. Paul mentions *one baptism* in Ephesians 4:5. He is not talking about immersion or sprinkling but about something that goes beyond that. When someone gives their heart to the Lord Jesus Christ, they are baptized by the Holy Spirit into the mystical body of Christ. The Church is the body with Christ as the head, and they are members of the body. Before they were ever baptized in water, they were baptized with the Holy Spirit of God into the body of Christ.

For by one Spirit we were all baptized into one body (1 Corinthians 12:13). This is what makes us one. We believe in water baptism, but water baptism symbolizes that which takes place when someone gives their heart to Jesus.

7. One God. We also worship one God—not Allah but Yahweh, Jehovah God. *One God and Father of all who is over all and through all and in all* (Ephesians 4:6). His name is Jehovah, and we cannot know Him apart from Jesus Christ. *No one comes to the Father but through Me* (John 14:6).

These are seven basic foundational truths that form and fashion our harmony and unity in the body of Christ. That is the **ground** of our unity. If we are going to build a spiritual house that passes the tests of time and trouble, we have to lay a firm and faithful foundation. As we strive to run the race toward the finish line, we seek to plant churches and make disciples and make this world more than a beautiful world but a saved world. The Apostle Paul articulated the seven pillars of our Christianity.

The Glory of Harmony Is Our Diversity

God made us one yet different all at the same time. *But to each one of us grace was given* (Ephesians 4:7). By using the word "but," Paul is changing direction. He had been talking about our sameness doctrinally; but then in contradiction, he used the word *But*. The Greek word for grace is "charis," a word from which we get "charismatic." *But to each one of us* [charisma] *was given according to the measure of Christ's gift* (Ephesians 4:7).

These are spiritual gifts. God made us, and not only do we have our unity but we also have diversity. What we have is unity in diversity.

I am not talking about diversity regarding doctrine. *Now I urge you, brethren, keep your eye on those who cause dissensions and hindrances contrary to the teaching which you learned, and turn away from them* (Romans 16:17). There is not room for every kind of belief, but there is room for people who have different gifts.

God gave us all different gifts that He might make us one, and we each have a grace gift. *But to each one of us grace* [charisma] *was given* (Ephesians 4:7). God gave us a gift to serve Him.

We may be divided over tastes but must not be divided over foundational doctrines.

My heart would be overwhelmed if every member of the Church were to discover, develop, and deploy their gift. Each of us has a spiritual gift, but it is not for our own ecstasy. It is not a toy; it is a tool.

Sameness is not unity. As a matter of fact, unity comes from diversity. My wife, Sheri, and I are quite different; but it is the difference that causes us to have unity.

One of the modern difficulties in the Church is we have different tastes also, such as in the styles of music we like to sing to praise the Lord. Some like it old, and some like new. Some like fast, and some like it slow. We may be divided over tastes but must not be divided over foundational doctrines.

There is glory in our diversity, and we are to celebrate that diversity. We are also to conserve our diversity. We do not all have to sing in unison.

The Goal of Harmony Is Our Maturity

Until we all attain to the unity of the faith, and of the knowledge of the Son of God, to a mature man, to the measure of the stature which belongs to the fullness of Christ (Ephesians 4:13).

Peace comes with unity, diversity, and maturity. Little children squabble and fuss; mature adults learn how to get along with one another. Bickering comes from immaturity; may God preserve the Church from bickering.

We are to be mature in **stature**. In order to know whether we are growing or not, we must not measure ourselves by a particular church leader but by Jesus Christ. The measure of our ministry is not based on the size of our buildings, budgets, or the number of Bible study attendees. The measuring stick is whether our team and our members are becoming more like Jesus Christ.

We are to be mature in **stability**. *As a result, we are no longer to be children, tossed here and there by waves and carried about by every wind of doctrine, by the trickery of men, by craftiness in deceitful scheming* (Ephesians 4:14). Get your feet on the rock. Paul told the church, *I know that after my departure savage wolves will come in among you, not sparing the flock* (Acts 20:29).

False cults do not produce converts nearly as much as they try to siphon off Bible believers who have no understanding. When immature believers are not rooted and grounded in the faith, they are drawn away into false doctrines because they are like little sailboats being blown this way and that way and being *carried about by every wind of doctrine* (Ephesians 4:14).

As mentioned earlier, we all must get a bulldog grip on the truth of these seven basic principles highlighted by Paul. We can be different in a lot of things; but when we grow up, we must be mature in stature and in stability.

We are to be mature in **speech**. *But speaking the truth in love, we are to grow up . . .* (Ephesians 4:15). We are not to speak truthless love or loveless truth. We are to speak the truth in love. Truth without love is brutality; love without truth is hypocrisy.

The Bible is a wonderful sword but a poor club. We are not to be a Bible bully, argumentative over the difference between Tweedledee and Tweedledum. We are never to jettison the truth but speak the truth in love.

We are not to speak truthless love or loveless truth.

We are to be mature in **service**. *From whom the whole body, being fitted and held together by what every joint supplies, according to the proper working of each individual part, causes the growth of the body for the building up of itself in love* (Ephesians 4:16).

Each part of what Paul teaches helps the other parts so that the whole body is healthy and growing and full of love. He speaks of the joints, and the Greek word for joint is "hamos," the word from which we get "harmony." The body is to work together and be flexible and coordinated. Each of us has a role in God's goal and a part in God's heart.

Our World in Christ

In the last three chapters, we discussed the basis of the unity of the church and the seven truths that are the seven pillars of our faith.

One of those great truths and the climatic truth of them all is that there is *one God and Father of all who is over all and through all and in all* (Ephesians 4:6).

God is the greatest subject ever; and while we will never know everything about God, there are some things we can know about Him. Following are some "God thoughts."

The Greatness of God

God is above all. There are many who do not even believe there is a God and others who say that it is difficult to believe. However, the opposite is actually true, for it is really impossible for a thinking person NOT to believe.

Those who do not believe in God feel that the universe is self-existing—that all matter came out of nothing. Once they believe that matter came out of nothing, they then believe that unaided, dead matter produced life—that there was a spontaneous combustion of life and that by sheer accident, living matter produced a mind. Their next step is to believe that the mind produced a conscience. In summary, out of chaos came the cosmos and out of disorder came order, and chance produced it all.

To think that matter came out of nothing and is self-existing is illogical.

Those who really believe that cannot be intellectually sound and must have unfurnished rooms to rent upstairs. To think that matter came out of nothing and is self-existing is illogical. To think that life came out of the dead, inanimate matter makes no sense for we know that there is a God who is above all.

George Gallup said, "I could prove God statistically. Take the human body alone—the chances that all the functions of an individual would just happen is a statistical monstrosity."

Scientists who research the human genome are in awe of the intricacies of the human body. Where there is design, there must be a designer.

For since the creation of the world His invisible attributes, His eternal power and divine nature, have been clearly seen, being understood through what has been made, so that they are without excuse (Romans 1:20).

For every house is built by someone, but the builder of all things is God (Hebrews 3:4)

A person who does not accept that God is above all is believing in a design without a designer, a creation without a creator, and an effect without a cause.

We do not have to understand God to experience God. We can see and feel the effect of God.

Electricity is an effect; and although we do not understand electricity, we certainly have no intention of sitting in the dark until we do. Before he died, Albert Einstein said he hoped to understand electricity but confessed that he never did. Therefore, it goes without saying that we do not have to understand God to experience God. We can see and feel the effect of God.

Dr. Edwin Conklin (November 24, 1863-November 20, 1952), a noted biologist, stated, "The probability of life originating from an accident is comparable to the probability of the unabridged dictionary resulting from an explosion in a printing shop."

Why do people refuse to believe in this God who is above all? *The fool has said in his heart, "There is no God"* (Psalm 14:1). The words, *There is*, is really saying, "The fool has said in his heart, no God." He simply does not want God; he refuses God. It is not a matter of the intellect; it is a matter of the heart.

The reason people do not want to believe in God is they do not want to be accountable to Him. *For even though they knew God, they did not honor Him as God or give thanks,* but they became futile in their speculations, and their foolish heart was darkened* (Romans 1:21).

It is not just what we say but what we do that has a lasting impact.

There is a story about an old Arab who had come to the end of his journey and the sun had already set. He got down off his camel, lit his lantern, reached into his knapsack, and pulled out one of three dates for his evening meal. He took the first date and held it up to the lantern and looked at it. It had a worm in it so he threw it over his shoulder into the sandy darkness. He reached into his knapsack and took out another date and held it up to the lantern. It had a worm in it as well so he threw it over his shoulder into the darkness. He then reached in the knapsack and pulled out the third date, blew out the lantern, and ate the date.

This is similar to what unbelievers do. They simply say, "I don't want the light to shine on me because I'm going to eat this date." They do not want the truth; therefore, they cannot find the truth which is that God is above all.

Many years ago, I read these words on a church sign: "Children spell love time." I will never forgot it. It is not just what we say but what we do that has a lasting impact.

Our heavenly Father could have ruled the universe without stepping on the earth, but then we would never have known Him or His love for us. He had to step out of eternity into time. The greatest step was not when Neil Armstrong placed his foot on the moon but when God placed His foot on the earth.

The Goodness of God

There is *one God and Father of all who is . . . through all* (Ephesians 4:6). Everything we receive comes through God.

By creation and by design, we can see that God is above all; but we really do not know the heart of God. If someone were to put a detective on my trail, he could find out some things about me but would never know me until I revealed myself to him. This reality is also true as it relates to God. We can find out some things about God by objective observation but can really only know the heart of God—the goodness of God—by revelation.

One of the greatest revelations that God has given of Himself is the names of God. *And those who know Your name will put their trust in You* (Psalm 9:10).

Elohim speaks of the **strength** of God. *In the beginning God created the heavens and the earth* (Genesis 1:1). The word for "God" is the word "Elohim." It is a combination of two words: "El" means unlimited strength and "allah" means covenant keeper.

This truth is found in the very first verse of the Bible. He is the God of infinite strength and absolute faithfulness who always keeps His word and with whom nothing is impossible.

For by him were all things created (Colossians 1:16). Jesus is Elohim. "In the beginning ***Elohim*** created the heavens and the earth." For by Jesus *all things were created, both in the heavens and on earth, visible and invisible, whether thrones or dominions or rulers or authorities—all things have been created through Him and for Him* (Colossians 1:16). God is through all; He is Elohim.

Jehovah—often translated "Lord God"—speaks of the **sovereignty** of God. God is through all (the goodness of God).

Our God is the God of strength and sovereignty.

When Moses asked God whom he should tell Pharaoh had sent him (Exodus 3:13), God told Moses *"I AM WHO I AM"; and He said, "Thus you shall say to the sons of Israel, 'I AM has sent me to you'"* (Exodus 3:14).

Jehovah means that God is the great I AM, the self-existing God. To the Jews, Jehovah, Yahweh (the self-existing God), the great I AM was the most sacred name. Many of the Jews would not even pronounce the name of God.

Just as Jesus is Elohim, He is also the great I AM. *Jesus said to them, "Truly, truly, I say to you, before Abraham was born, I am"* (John 8:58).

Jesus did not begin in Bethlehem. *In the beginning was the Word, and the Word was with God, and the Word was God* (John 1:1). Our God is the God of strength and sovereignty.

Adonai—one who is master, who is superior, and who is Lord over us—speaks of the **superiority** of God. *Then Moses said to the Lord, "Please, Lord [Adonai], I have never been eloquent, neither recently nor in time past, nor since You have spoken to Your servant; for I am slow of speech and slow of tongue* (Exodus 4:10).

Jesus Christ (He is Lord of all) (Acts 10:36). In the name of Jesus are all of the attributes of the eternal God compounded into one precious name—the name of Jesus.

El Shaddai—God Almighty—speaks of the **sufficiency** of God. The word "El" means almighty or powerful and "Shaddai" comes from a word that means breast. Like a woman's breast, it speaks of sufficiency. All a baby needs for sustenance is in the mother's breast. This is one of the most beautiful pictures of God in the Bible because it is great strength mingled with complete sufficiency.

Abraham was 99 years old, and his reproductive abilities were decimated. There was no way he could father a child, but God had promised him a child in his old age. When God appeared to Abraham, the name He used was El Shaddai—the God who is sufficient.

Jesus is El Shaddai—the one who nurtures us and from whom we receive life. *I am the vine, you are the branches* (John 15:5). He is our sustenance, our strength, and our sufficiency.

El Elyon—the Most High God, the strongest of the strong, the highest of the high—speaks of the **supremacy** of God. Abraham met a man named Melchizedek, *and Melchizedek king of Salem* [the word Salem means peace] *brought out bread and wine; now he was a priest of God. He blessed him and said, "Blessed be Abram of God Most High, Possessor of heaven and earth And blessed be God Most High, Who has delivered your enemies into your hand." He* [Abraham] *gave him* [Melchizedek] *a tenth of all* (Genesis 14:18-19). In Hebrews 7, Melchizedek is a picture and type of the Lord Jesus Christ.

Jesus is our El Elyon. *For by Him all things were created, both in the heavens and on earth, visible and invisible, whether thrones or dominions or rulers or authorities—all things have been created through Him and for Him. He is before all things, and in Him all things hold together* (Colossians 1:16-17). He is above all things.

El Olam — the everlasting God — speaks of the **stability** of God. *Lord, You have been our dwelling place in all generations. Before the mountains were born or You gave birth to the earth and the world, even from everlasting to everlasting, You are God* (Psalm 90:1-2). What a wonderful truth to know that in a changing world, God never changes.

There are no surprises to God, no panic in heaven.

The eternal God is a dwelling place, and underneath are the everlasting arms; and He drove out the enemy from before you, and said, "Destroy!" (Deuteronomy 33:27). Time does not alter God. *For a thousand years in Your sight are like yesterday when it passes by, or as a watch in the night* (Psalm 90:4). There are no surprises to God, no panic in heaven. He is the everlasting God and knows the past and the future all at the same time.

Jesus is our El Olam, the King of the Ages. *But of the Son He says, "Your throne, O God, is forever and ever, And the righteous scepter is the scepter of His kingdom* (Hebrews 1:8).

El Roi — the God who sees — speaks of the **sympathy** of God.

This name was first revealed by Hagar, Sarah's Egyptian handmaiden. At Sarah's behest, Abraham took Hagar as his wife; and she became pregnant. Sarah tried to help God out; but that was not God's plan. Hagar became pregnant by Abraham; and *Sarai treated her harshly, and she fled from her presence* (Genesis 16:6). While Hagar was fleeing in the wilderness, friendless and homeless, God had compassion on her. An angel appeared to Hagar to give her direction and to speak of God's grace and mercy. *Then she called the name of the Lord who spoke to her, "You are a God who sees"; for she said, "Have I even remained alive here after seeing Him?* (Genesis 16:13).

We must never forget that God sees us and knows our very thoughts and imaginations. There is no heartache, pain, or trouble that He does not know. *Behold, the eye of the Lord is on those who fear Him, on those who hope for His lovingkindness* (Psalm 33:18). *For we do not have a high priest who cannot sympathize with our weaknesses* (Hebrews 4:15).

He is the God of strength—Elohim. He is the God of sovereignty—Jehovah. He is the God of superiority—Adonai. He is the God of sufficiency—El Shaddai. He is the God of supremacy—El Elyon. He is the God of stability—El Olam. He is the God of sympathy—El Roi. All of these names are wrapped up in one name—the name of Jesus which is a name that is above every name!

God is above all, and that speaks of the **greatness** of God. God is through all, and that speaks of the **goodness** of God.

The Grace of God

There is *one God and Father of all who is over all and through all and in all* (Ephesians 4:6). The God who is above all is also the God who is through all as well as the God who is in all. How wonderful that this great and good God will live in us. This is nothing short of **amazing grace**.

Paul is talking about the unity of the church. We are all a little peculiar and different. If it were not for Jesus, we would not and could not stay together; yet there is that wonderful unity because we are all a part of the family of God! Our Lord is adding more than 120,000 new family members each day throughout the world!

8

Our Wealth in Christ

Outside of the Apostle Paul, many key Christian leaders believe Charles Spurgeon, pastor of Metropolitan Tabernacle in London, England, was the greatest preacher who ever lived. On one occasion, Spurgeon told a very moving story of an extremely poor woman who had been a member of his congregation and lived in slum-type housing.

Pastor Spurgeon went to visit her to give her some comfort and help. While he was there, he looked up and saw a framed legal document on the wall and walked over and read it carefully. It was a document transferring amazing wealth to this woman. She didn't even know what it was and had framed it and put it on her wall!

What had happened was that she had taken care of an elderly man; and when he died, he left her his estate. Unfortunately, she was an uneducated woman and did not know what it was. When the bank finally learned about this, they said, "We wondered who the old gentlemen had left his estate to."

I think of the incredible inheritance the Lord Jesus Christ left us when He ascended to heaven.

When I think of this story, I think of the incredible inheritance the Lord Jesus Christ left us when He ascended to heaven. We need to learn and to live in this inheritance!

It may be that you have not yet discovered what you have in the Lord Jesus. Could it be that you have framed your spiritual gift as a motto on the wall rather than having carried it to the bank to cash it and use it? Or could it be that you have left your gift under the tree, wrapped and unopened and, therefore, unappreciated?

When God saved you, He saved you by His grace, but He did not save you to sit, soak, and sour. He saved you to serve. *But to each one of us grace was given according to the measure of Christ's gift* (Ephesians 4:7).

God has given you a spiritual gift. *But to each one of us grace was given.* The word "grace" is the Greek word "charis" from which we get the word "charismatic." You have a charismatic gift; however, do not think by charismatic that we mean someone who has a ready smile, a firm handshake, and verbal ability. We say, "Well, that man is charismatic. He'd make a good politician." That is a corruption of the word charismatic. The word charismatic merely means a person who has been gifted by grace. *But to each one of us grace* [charis] *was given according to the measure of Christ's gift* (Ephesians 4:7).

You are a gifted child, but you may be like that poor woman who did not understand what the gift that she had received was and did not know how to use it. Therefore, we want to examine how to discover, develop, and deploy your spiritual gift and minister in the body of Christ.

How the Gifts Are Delivered

The first truth we need to learn is how the gifts are delivered. *But to each one of us grace was given according to the measure of Christ's gift* (Ephesians 4:7).

God has given you a grace gift; therefore, do not insult Him by saying He cannot use you. In the church, there can be no inferiority or superiority. We are what we are by the gift of God.

Everyone has a charismatic gift—a grace gift. A charismatic gift is a God-given ability for service and ministry. However, it goes beyond natural talent. Spiritual gifts are supernatural—supernatural in source, supernatural in nature, and supernatural in purpose.

You do not choose your spiritual gifts any more than you choose your natural gifts. You can develop your natural talents, but you did not choose them any more than you chose the color of your eyes or the color of your skin. You received them genetically by your first birth, and your talents are genetically encoded in you by that first birth. However, spiritual gifts are given at your new birth and are supernatural.

The gifts are given by the ascended Lord. *Therefore it says, "When He [Jesus] ascended on high, He led captive a host of captives [the devil], And He gave gifts to men [you]." (Now this expression, "He ascended," what does it mean except that He also had descended into the lower parts of the earth?* (Ephesians 4:8-9).

The Lord Jesus descended—He came to this earth, lived a perfect life, suffered, bled, died on the cross, was buried, and rose again. When Jesus Christ died on the cross for us and with His blood purchased our salvation, at the same time He broke Satan's back. Satan's kingdom came crashing down, and he and his malevolent forces were demolished at Calvary.

Satan had taken the world captive, but Jesus took Satan captive.

Therefore, by His death, burial, resurrection, and ascension, the Lord Jesus Christ led captivity captive. Satan had taken the world captive, but Jesus took Satan captive.

The Apostle Paul was talking about a Roman triumph. When a Roman general would win a battle for Rome, he would come back into the city for a parade called "The Triumph." The air would be filled with incense and perfume, and he would be riding on his white horse. The priests would be swinging incense and perfume and the people would be giving their praises to the general.

Behind the general would be the conquered kings and generals who would have been stripped naked and chained to the conquering general's chariot wheels. They would be dragged along behind the chariot while the people jeered and mocked those who had been stripped, shamed, and subdued. Their power was gone and their pride lay in the dust. Behind them would be servants bearing all of the spoils of the battle, the riches that had been conquered and brought back to Rome.

The Lord Jesus ascended on high and led captivity captive. Satan's kingdom was ruined and the spoils of the battle—our grace gifts to serve our great King—given to us. Never despise or overlook your grace gifts. They are spiritual gifts from our conqueror, the Lord Jesus Christ, who paid an unimaginable price for us.

How the Gifts Are Described

Now there are varieties of gifts, but the same Spirit (1 Corinthians 12:4). It is the Holy Spirit who gives different gifts to the church. *And there are varieties of ministries, and the same Lord* (1 Corinthians 12:5). Everything is not always done the same way, but it is the Lord who is doing it. *There are varieties of effects, but the same God who works all things in all persons. But to each one is given the manifestation of the Spirit for the common good* (1 Corinthians 4:6-7).

God gave you a spiritual gift, not for your own enjoyment but for your employment. Your spiritual gift is to bless the church, not to bless you. It is a tool, not a toy.

*For to one is given the word of **wisdom*** (1 Corinthians 12:8). The word of wisdom is supernatural insight into the mind of God. It is not talking about common sense but about uncommon sense. People who have the gift of the word of wisdom make wonderful counselors.

*And to another the word of **knowledge*** (1 Corinthians 12:8). Knowledge differs from wisdom in that it is the supernatural ability to know and apply the things of God. Knowledge puts wisdom to practical use. Some will have the gift of wisdom and some the gift of knowledge. Those who have both gifts make wonderful leaders and counselors.

*To another **faith** by the same Spirit* (1 Corinthians 12:9). All believers have faith or they could not be called believers for no one can be saved without faith; however, some people have the supernatural gift of faith—mountain-moving faith. These kinds of people are the visionaries and the pioneers, those who are able to think big and believe God for great things.

And to another gifts of **healing** *by the one Spirit* (1 Corinthians 12:9). Note that it states gifts of healings—plural. There are healings for the body, soul, and mind—physical healing, spiritual healing, and psychological healing.

Every church ought to pray for God to give prophets to the church—those who can speak for God.

And to another the effecting of **miracles** (1 Corinthians 12:10). We cannot deny that God is a God of might and miracle.

And to another **prophecy** (1 Corinthians 12:10). This is the ability to foretell and forth tell—primarily not to foretell the future but to tell forth the will of God in a particular matter. We do not have to guess about what the gift of prophecy is because we are told the *one who prophesies speaks to men for edification and exhortation and consolation* (1 Corinthians 14:3). Edification means to build people up as in building a building—an edifice—while exhortation means to encourage, exhort, cheer, and fire people up. Consolation means to comfort or hold people up. A prophet is someone who builds up, fires up, and shores up the people of God. Every church ought to pray for God to give prophets to the church—those who can speak for God.

And to another the **distinguishing of spirits** (1 Corinthians 12:10). There are a lot of wild and wicked spirits in the world today.

*To another **various kinds of tongues*** (1 Corinthians 12:10). This means the ability to praise God in a language never learned. When someone speaks in tongues in a worship service, the Lord also desires that the message be interpreted in order for the people to be able to understand it so He gave the gift of *the **interpretation of tongues**.*

Since we have gifts that differ according to the grace given to us, each of us is to exercise them accordingly: if prophecy according to the proportion of his faith (Romans 12:6). Ministry is an act of service.

*God has appointed in the church ... **teachers*** (1 Corinthians 12:28). If you have the gift of teaching, then you should be teaching a class or a group.

*Since we have gifts that differ according to the grace given to us, each of us is to exercise them accordingly ... he who exhorts, in his **exhortation*** (Romans 12:6,8). Gifted musicians who have not only vocal ability but also the ability to move the heart often have the gift of exhortation as well as those who do visitation.

Since we have gifts that differ according to the grace given to us, each of us is to exercise them accordingly ... he who gives, with liberality (Romans 12:6,8). This is the gift of **giving** which is the supernatural ability to make and give money sacrificially and wisely.

Since we have gifts that differ according to the grace given to us, each of us is to exercise them accordingly ... he who leads, with diligence (Romans 12:6,8). This is the gift of **leading**. We need people who can head up committees and those who can administrate and lead people forward in various ministries.

*Since we have gifts that differ according to the grace given to us, each of us is to exercise them accordingly ... he who shows **mercy**, with cheerfulness* (Romans 12:6,8). These are people who do hospital visitation and serve in benevolence ministries.

We all have a role in the goal and a part in God's heart!

How the Gifts Are Developed

And He gave some as apostles, and some as prophets, and some as evangelists, and some as pastors and teachers, for the equipping of the saints for the work of service, to the building up of the body of Christ (Ephesians 4:11-12). Not only does God give spiritual gifts to everyone, but He also gives spiritual leaders to the church.

The fivefold ministry gifts are not only representative of distinct people and ministerial offices in the church, but they also reveal five principles for effective ministry today.

The fivefold ministry gifts are not only representative of distinct people and ministerial offices in the church, but they also reveal five principles for effective ministry today. The apostle, prophet, evangelist, pastor, and teacher represent the principles of governing, guiding, gathering, guarding, and garnering, respectively. All of these principles are needed for equipping Christians for effective evangelism.

In the early church, there was not much difference between an apostle and an evangelist since all apostles were also evangelists. However, not all evangelists were apostles since a direct call by the Lord was necessary. John Calvin believed there were times when God would raise up evangelists as substitutes for apostles. In a real sense, "the apostles did not know when to stop being evangelists." Without the ministry of the true New Testament evangelist, the church would die out.

In Ephesians 4:11, the evangelist seems to "denote an order of workers midway between apostles and prophets on the one hand and pastors and teachers on the other." There has been much scholarly debate as to whether the ministry gifts consist of four or five separate entities. This debate is the result of the definite article being present before all the various leadership gifts except "teachers" (*toùs dè poiménas kai didaskálous*). The one definite article for both pastors and teachers indicates the "close association of functions between two types of ministers who operate within the local congregation." Even though there is an obvious association between pastor and teacher, there are also distinctives in ministry (Acts 13:1; Romans 12:7; 1 Corinthians 12:28). This interpretation is paralleled in contemporary ministry.

Sometimes these ministerial gifts (Ephesians 4:11) did overlap in the early church. For example, Paul functioned not only as an apostle but also as a prophet, evangelist, pastor, and teacher. Christ used Paul in a fivefold gifting of itinerant evangelistic ministry. For Paul, "the work of the ministry is of much greater importance than any hierarchy of officials."

The aim of all ministry gifts in Ephesians 4:11 is for the equipping of God's people for the *work of service, to the building up of the body of Christ* (Ephesians 4:12). The Greek term for equipping (*katartismòn*) means to put right or to put in order. In surgery, it is applied to the setting of a broken bone. Equipping denotes "the bringing of the saints to a condition of fitness for the discharge of their functions in the body, without implying restoration from a disordered state. The evangelist, along with the other four ministry gifts, is to set the local church in order, making each member fit for the work of ministry. In the case of the evangelist, this 'work of service' or 'ministry' is equipping for evangelism." For the local church to be active in evangelism, the body of Christ must be spiritually healthy.

The Greek term for "building up" (*oikodomēn*) refers "to the act of building . . . to build on something, to build further." There is a fourfold equipping or maturing function for the evangelist in the church. Even though not specially stated, these functions are easily applied to the pastor's leadership roles in the local church. For evangelists and pastors to function biblically, their message, motives, methods, and ministry must align with the Christ-given purposes outlined in Ephesians 4:13-16.

If you want God to use you, you must stop just praying for God to use you and become usable.

If you want God to use you, you must stop just praying for God to use you and become usable. God will then wear you out. Following are five principles to knowing your spiritual gift:

1. **Desire.** What do you enjoy doing? What do you do naturally? What do you feel you do well?
2. **Discovery.** You will discover your gift as you endeavor to do it. Other people will say, "You have the ability to lead in this area." Dr. Harry Ironside who pastored Moody Church in Chicago from 1929 to 1948 used to say, "It's a sad thing to hear a man who thinks he has the gift of preaching when no one else has the gift of listening."
3. **Development.** You need to stir up the gift of God. Paul told Timothy to *be diligent to present yourself approved to God as a workman who does not need to be*

ashamed, accurately handling the word of truth (Timothy 2:15). Your spiritual gift must be developed.
4. **Dependence.** Your spiritual gift must operate in the power of the Holy Spirit. Since your spiritual gifts are supernatural, they operate with supernatural power.
5. **Deployment.** You must put your spiritual gift to work by working with other saints. Your gift is significant as it relates to other gifted people.

How the Gifts Are Displayed

What happens when you find your ministry? *We all attain to the unity of the faith, and of the knowledge of the Son of God, to a mature man, to the measure of the stature which belongs to the fullness of Christ* (Ephesians 4:13). When these gifts work together, the body matures and becomes like its head, the Lord Jesus Christ.

This fivefold leadership team is to help the church become mature in **stature**. Their ministry is to be active *until we all attain to the unity of the faith, and of the knowledge of the Son of God, to a mature man, to the measure of the stature which belongs to the fullness of Christ* (Ephesians 4:13). This verse paints a picture of the church maturing into a perfect, full-grown man (*eis ándra téleion*). "This perfection or completeness is proportionate to the fullness of Christ himself." The whole body of Christ is viewed as one new man with one faith in the Son of God. *The faith* is the full message of the gospel. *The measure of the stature* (*métron hēlikías*) indicates a level of spiritual perfection found in the fullness of Christ. The body of Christ is seen as progressing toward its goal of perfection in the fullness of Christ. In short, as Christ inhabits our humanity, we are to display His deity.

This leadership team can help the local church mature in **stability**. *We are no longer to be children, tossed here and there by waves and carried about by every wind of doctrine, by the trickery of men, by craftiness in deceitful scheming* (Ephesians 4:14). In Ephesians 4:13-14, there is a purposeful contrast made between *a mature man* and "children." Instead of spiritual maturity, the picture is of "spiritual infantilism." The immature Christian is "swung around" by the wind and waves of "fashionable heterodoxy." Instability is one definite sign of immaturity.

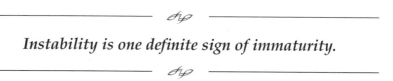

Instability is one definite sign of immaturity.

The Apostle Paul knew a lot about being tossed back and forth on the sea, yet it is far worse for Christians to be "whirled around by every gust of doctrine." The concept that Paul teaches is not "physical infants in a boat who are helpless to manage it in waves and wind; but of physical men, who know nothing about managing boats, who are infants amid wind and waves."

This leadership team can help the local church mature in **speech**. *Speaking the truth in love, we are to grow up in all aspects into Him who is the head, even Christ* (Ephesians 4:15). *Speaking the truth* (*alētheúontes*) means "truthing" or "doing the truth" (Wood, 11:59). A mature church does not tolerate error. Mature Christians recognize religious tricksters by comparing them to the truth. They correct the error of these religious charlatans by speaking the truth in love. "Truthing in love" keeps *every joint* (Ephesians 4:16) limber and flexible in the midst of a changing culture. It has been said, "Whatever is in the well of the heart comes out in the bucket of speech." When the heart of the body of

Christ is filled with truth and love, Christians will lovingly speak out against all errors in their society.

This leadership team can help the local church mature in **service**. *From whom the whole body, being fitted and held together by what every joint supplies, according to the proper working of each individual part, causes the growth of the body for the building up of itself in love* (Ephesians 4:16). The ultimate goal of an active, fivefold ministry is a "coordinated body with each member fulfilling his function." This maturing process depends on the truth that the various ministries in Ephesians 4:11 are interrelated.

Each ministry gift should embrace the other for the dual purpose of equipping the church and evangelizing the lost.

The whole body of Christ is being "fitted together" and "held together" by each separate "joint." The Greek term for *supplies* (épichorēgías) is derived from *choregos*. He "was the man who met the cost of staging a Greek play with its chorus." It is only when every aspect of the fivefold ministries is working together that the body of Christ receives the full support it needs to do the "work of service." The lifeblood of the body of Christ is love. Each member is to have a loving heart toward the other members of the body of Christ.

The fivefold ministries of the church are to function like an ensemble singing its various parts. They should produce a harmonic sound throughout the church. Moreover, each ministry joint should be limber, not stiff or limited by spiritual arthritis. Each ministry gift should embrace the other for the dual purpose of equipping the church and evangelizing the lost. When the evangelist is biblically, spiritually, and creatively functioning in the contemporary church, the whole body of Christ is more mature in stature, stability, speech, and service.

When I studied human anatomy and physiology in college, I found that we have synovial fluid that lubricates these joints. When the cartilage gets dry and the synovial fluid is not there and the joint gets inflamed, swollen, stiff, and painful, then the body is not lubricated.

What is the synovial fluid? Love. When we love one another, we do not inflame one another, we do get stiff, we do not become rigid. We all have our gifts of God. We become mature in stature—we become like Christ. We become mature in stability—we are not blown about. We become mature in speech—we know how to speak the truth in love. We become mature in service—we serve one another. The body works together!

Our Wins in Christ

There are people who have satanic strongholds in their lives which are not only harming them and wrecking their spiritual life but are also contaminating the lives of their family and the life of their church. The devil has found an unclean place in that person and has made a campground—a foul nest, a beachhead, a citadel, a stronghold; and the devil uses that stronghold to war against God and against the work of God.

Neither give place to the devil (Ephesians 4:27) . . . *and grieve not the holy Spirit of God* (Ephesians 4:30). These two verses are shocking and frightening and ought to cause every one of us to sit up and take notice that we—saved, born-again children of God—could give place to the devil or grieve the Holy Spirit of God.

Once you have given place to the devil, he is going to work on you for the rest of your life. Suppose you had 50 acres of land and decided to sell me one acre in the middle of those 50 acres. You have also given me ingress and egress across your property. However, on my one acre, I play loud music all night long, throw trash around, and do everything I can to desecrate the property. You finally say to me, "I want you out! You're desecrating the property and defiling the area!"

Every area where there is unconfessed sin is legal ground for Satan.

My response is, "I'm not going. I don't have to go, and you can't make me go. You sold this piece of property to me, and I've got a legal right to it. I am not moving."

The bottom line is that you would not be able to move me out because you gave me a legal place there. There are a lot of Christians who have done almost the same thing with Satan. They have given place to the devil and cannot dislodge him unless they legally dislodge him. Over time, those strongholds became habitual things in their lives; and they will have to take three legal steps to get him out.

There must be **repentance.** *You lay aside the old self, which is being corrupted in accordance with the lusts of deceit* (Ephesians 4:22). The words *lay aside* mean "put away, be done with it." You have to confess it, forsake it, and deal with it. There is only one thing to do with sin, and that is to repent.

Not only must there be repentance, but there must also be **resistance.** *Do not give the devil an opportunity* (Ephesians 4:27). What you gave to him you must take back, but you can never take it back until you take away his legal authority and that legal authority is the sin in your life.

Every area where there is unconfessed sin is legal ground for Satan. Until you confess that sin, Satan has every right to make a campground there.

Repentance and resistance are not enough though. There must also be **renewal**. *And that you be renewed in the spirit of your mind, and put on the new self, which in the likeness of God has been created in righteousness and holiness of the truth* (Ephesians 4:23-24).

We Must Have Repentance

A text without a context is but a pretext. The verses surrounding Ephesians 4:27 warns about giving place to the devil.

1. Lying. *Therefore, laying aside falsehood, SPEAK TRUTH EACH ONE of you WITH HIS NEIGHBOR, for we are members of one another* (Ephesians 4:25). If you are a liar or if your life is not based on absolute, total, impeccable truth, then you have created a climate where the devil will feel welcome.

The devil's nature is lying. Jesus said that the devil *is a liar and the father of lies* (John 8:44). If you really want the devil to feel at home in your life, you should live a lie, love a lie, and believe a lie. He is the prince of darkness, and lying is in the realm of darkness. On the other hand, God's kingdom is built on truth. Jesus said that He is *the truth* (John 14:6), *Your word is truth* (John 17:17), and *the Spirit is the truth* (1 John 5:6).

If there is any area of your life that is not impeccably, indisputably, and completely honest, then that will be the devil's campground. Remember that you can lie with the tone of your voice or just by arching your eyebrows.

2. Stealing. If there is thievery in your life, that is a climate that Satan loves because Satan is a thief.

If you would steal so much as a 15-cent pencil and carry it home from the job, you have made a place for the devil. *He who is faithful in a very little thing is faithful also in much; and he who is unrighteous in a very little thing is unrighteous also in much* (Luke 16:10). With God, thievery is thievery no matter the monetary amount.

If you are not a tither, then you are a thief. *Will a man rob God? Yet you are robbing Me! But you say, "How have we robbed You?" In tithes and offerings* (Malachi 3:8). Everything we have belongs to God.

Filthy speech makes room for the devil.

---

3. **Filthy Speech.** Filthy speech makes room for the devil. *Let no unwholesome word proceed from your mouth, but only such a word as is good for edification according to the need of the moment, so that it will give grace to those who hear* (Ephesians 4:29).

There must be no filthiness and silly talk, or coarse jesting, which are not fitting, but rather giving of thanks (Ephesians 5:4). Not only is the devil a thief, but he is also filthy.

Let no unwholesome word proceed from your mouth, but only such a word as is good for edification (Ephesians 4:29). There is a certain kind of language—a certain kind of talk—as well as certain kinds of stories that are filthy and do not build up but instead tear down, destroy, and desecrate. If you have a foul, filthy mouth and tell these kinds of stories, it is because you have a filthy heart; and a filthy heart is a place where Satan incubates and dwells. He will wreck and ruin your life and make a stronghold out of it.

4. **Bitterness.** Bitterness creates a climate for the devil. *Do not grieve the Holy Spirit of God, by whom you were sealed for*

the day of redemption. Let all bitterness and wrath and anger and clamor and slander be put away from you, along with all malice (Ephesians 4:30-31).

The devil has bitterness and a vendetta against the nation of Israel, God's holy people (Revelation 12:12-17). If you are bitter, then you are like the devil; and if you are not careful, you will become evil.

The devil loves to find a bitter heart. If you are a bitter person, then you have no joy in your heart. You can sit in church with a smile on your face, but your prayers are not getting through to God and you are contaminating the lives of those around you. You are giving place to the devil.

5. Slander. *Let all bitterness and wrath and anger and clamor and slander be put away from you, along with all malice* (Ephesians 4:31). Bitterness often leads to slander. The devil is called *the accuser of our brethren* (Revelation 12:10), and his name means "slanderer." If you are a slanderer or a gossip or if you are speaking evil, then you are literally doing the devil's work.

6. Malice. *Let all bitterness and wrath and anger and clamor and slander be put away from you, along with all malice* (Ephesians 4:31). Someone did you wrong, and you feel wounded. The devil brings bitterness into your life; and after a while, the bitterness turns to wrath. The Greek word for *wrath* has the idea of something that burns on the inside—like an internal heat or smoldering rags in an attic or a closet. If you do not deal with the bitterness, you will begin to have a slow burn. After a while, those smoldering rags burst into flames and show up as anger. That which was internal becomes external.

But the devil is not finished yet. The anger then turns to *clamor* (meaning "to speak loudly"), and the clamor turns to "evil speaking." It is the picture of a person who lets another person "really have it" verbally and begins to say things they really do not mean and had never even really thought of—expressions such as, "I hate you"; "You'll never amount to anything"; "I wish I had never met you"; "I wish we had never gotten married"; I wish you were dead."

God will not accept an alibi or an excuse for sin.

This path ends up with *malice* (meaning "a desire to hurt somebody"). After the evil speaks, you just want to shake the person. This path lets the devil come in; however, the devil can take no place except what we give him.

All along, the Holy Spirit is weeping and is heartbroken. We can indeed break the heart of God. It is the same as a picture of parents grieving over their children. *Do not grieve the Holy Spirit of God* (Ephesians 4:30). It is hard to imagine our "temple" which has been saved, redeemed, born again, and purchased with the blood of Jesus becoming a nest of Satan.

We are not going to get that place back until we repent. God will not accept an alibi or an excuse for sin. There must be repentance, and repentance is not just being broken *over* our sin; it is being broken *from* our sin. It must be put away and done with. *You lay aside the old self, which is being corrupted in accordance with the lusts of deceit* (Ephesians 4:22).

We Must Have Resistance

Even after there is repentance, there can be resistance. The devil is not just going to walk out; you must run him out. *Resist the devil and he will flee from you* (James 4:7). If you do not resist him, he will not go.

Even when you repent, you must still clean house. You must go in with a power of attorney which is the name of Jesus and take the land by saying, "I clean it out. I repent of the sin. It's all done, devil. You have no more rights. You have no more legal authority." You can then take the blood of Jesus Christ as your authority and Christ as your attorney.

You can say to Satan in no uncertain terms, "I have given you place, but I take it back in the name and the authority of Jesus. I bring Jesus Christ against you. You have no right; you have no authority. This body of mine is the temple of the Holy Spirit of God, and you are trespassing on my Father's property. In the name of Jesus, whose I am and whom I serve, be gone!" And he will flee from you.

If you try to resist the devil with unconfessed sin in your heart and life, he will laugh in your face and make a mockery of you. You will say, "Devil, leave me alone"; and he will say, "Ha, who do you think you are? You gave me this piece of property, and I am not moving out." There must be repentance, and then there can be resistance.

We Must Have Renewal

And that you be renewed in the spirit of your mind, and put on the new self, which in the likeness of God has been created in righteousness and holiness of the truth (Ephesians 4:23-24). It is not enough to put off the old man; God wants us to know true holiness. *Do not grieve the Holy Spirit of God, by whom you were sealed for the day of redemption* (Ephesians 4:30).

And do not get drunk with wine, for that is dissipation, but be filled with the Spirit (Ephesians 5:18). We have a choice — we can grieve the Spirit of God and be filled with the devil, or we can put the devil out and be filled with the Spirit of God. There is no place for the devil when you are filled with the Spirit.

There is no place for the devil when you are filled with the Spirit.

What does it mean to *be filled with the Spirit*? The Holy Spirit is not some sort of a liquid, and you are not a jug. You are the temple of the Holy Spirit in person. To *be filled with the Spirit* means that there is not one room in your temple that is off-limits to Him. There is not one closet to which He does not have a key.

When you are filled with the Spirit, He impacts your business life, political life, church life, and social life as well as big things and little things including money, exercise, eating, sleeping, and waking. "Jesus, I give you the keys to it all. I am filled with the Spirit." And when you are filled with the Spirit, there is no more room for Satan. If there is room for Satan, then the Spirit is grieved and you are not filled with the Spirit (Ephesians 4:30).

Our Wage in Christ

There are two problems that do great psychological, emotional, and spiritual damage: guilt and bitterness. Guilt imprisons us, and bitterness poisons us. Forgiveness is the answer to both. Guilt is the result of something we have done wrong, and bitterness is our reaction to someone else's wrong or our perception that someone else has wronged us. Both put us in a prison, but it is God's forgiveness of us that sets us free from the prison of guilt and our forgiveness of others that sets us free from the prison of bitterness.

> *Let all bitterness and wrath and anger and clamor and slander be put away from you, along with all malice. Be kind to one another, tender-hearted, forgiving each other, just as God in Christ also has forgiven you* (Ephesians 4:31-32).

When we truly forgive someone, we set two people free: the person we have forgiven and ourselves.

It is God's forgiveness of us that sets us free from the prison of guilt and our forgiveness of others that sets us free from the prison of bitterness.

To forgive means "to pay a debt." This is the reason our Lord taught us to pray: *And forgive us our debts, as we also have forgiven our debtors* (Matthew 6:12). Sin is a debt we owe. We have sinned against heaven and the kingdom of God and have been sued for damages, but it is a debt we cannot pay. However, in mercy and in love, God has forgiven us and paid that debt; but there are no free pardons. When someone is forgiven, someone else has paid.

In Him we have redemption through His blood, the forgiveness of our trespasses, according to the riches of His grace (Ephesians 1:7). Out of the riches of His grace, He paid the debt. That is the reason we call *salvation* "grace" —G-R-A-C-E: "**G**od's **R**iches **A**t **C**hrist's **E**xpense."

Once we are in God's family, we must learn to practice the forgiveness of others because if we do not, we are going to dam up the stream of God's mercy. When we get saved, we are in the family; however, if we fail to forgive others, we will destroy family fellowship.

The Compelling Reasons for Forgiveness

1. The grace factor. *Be kind to one another, tender-hearted, forgiving each other, just as God in Christ also has forgiven you* (Ephesians 4:32). If I have been sinned against, why should I forgive? Because God forgave me when I sinned against Him. He willingly, lovingly, and freely forgives us. We call that grace.

Those who refuse to forgive destroy the bridge over which they must travel.

2. The guilt factor. Jesus said, *For if you forgive others for their transgressions, your heavenly Father will also forgive you. But if you do not forgive others, then your Father will not forgive your transgressions* (Matthew 6:14–15). Those who refuse to forgive destroy the bridge over which they must travel. An unforgiving spirit is unforgivable. Forgiving and being forgiven go together.

And forgive us our debts, as we also have forgiven our debtors (Matthew 6:12). If we do not intend to forgive the person who has wronged us, then Matthew 6:12 is a very foolish prayer to pray. What we are really praying is, "Father, treat me like I treat others and forgive me in the same manner that I forgive them." But what we are actually praying is, "I am not going to forgive the other person so don't forgive me," or "Well, I'll forgive her, but I'll never have anything more to do with her" so God says, "Okay. I'll forgive you but will never have anything more to do with you either." In this manner, we are asking God to "forgive us in the same manner that we forgive those who sin against us."

Jesus illustrated this truth with a story. *For this reason the kingdom of heaven may be compared to a king who wished to settle accounts with his slaves. When he had begun to settle them, one who owed him ten thousand talents was brought to him* (Matthew 18:23-24).

The story is about a king who was taking inventory and finds that a man owes him ten thousand talents. *But since he did not have the means to repay, his lord commanded him to be sold, along with his wife and children and all that he had, and repayment to be made. So the slave fell to the ground and prostrated himself before him, saying, "Have patience with me and I will repay you everything." And the lord of that slave felt compassion and released him and forgave him the debt* (Matthew 18:25-27).

The Lord is saying, "It is absolutely wicked for those of us who have been forgiven so much to refuse to forgive someone else."

When Jesus said, *ten thousand talents*, He was talking about an enormous debt. A *talent* was the largest measure of money known in the Roman world and would equal 60 million denarii or 60 million days of work. It was an astronomical amount of money for the common man, an unforgivable debt; however; the king forgave him and, by doing so, cost himself ten thousand talents.

We then find that the man who had been forgiven millions of dollars' worth of debt goes out and finds someone who owes him a hundred days' wages. *But that slave went out and found one of his fellow slaves who owed him a hundred denarii; and he seized him and began to choke him, saying, "Pay back what you owe." So his fellow slave fell to the ground and began to plead with him, saying, 'Have patience with me and I will repay you.' But he was unwilling and went and threw him in prison until he should pay back what was owed* (Matthew 18:28-30).

Jesus made an analogy of the wickedness of the man who had been forgiven but would not forgive. *And his lord, moved with anger, handed him over to the torturers until he should repay all that was owed him. My heavenly Father will also do the same to you, if each of you does not forgive his brother from your heart* (Matthew 34-35). The Lord is saying, "It is absolutely wicked for those of us who have been forgiven so much to refuse to forgive someone else."

3. The grief factor. The grief factor is a reason we ought to forgive because the man who failed to forgive endured the severest of discipline. *See to it that no one comes short of the grace of God; that no root of bitterness springing up causes trouble, and by it many be defiled* (Hebrews 12:15). If we do not forgive, we are going to know unusual grief and be troubled as are others around us.

Some miscreant has done something bad to us, and we say, "Look what he did to me! I'm going to get even." If we do, we come down to his level so we begin to think it over and then say, "Okay, I won't get even; I'll just continue to hate him." If we do that, we will then be committing emotional suicide by filling ourselves with bitterness which is an acid that will destroy us and hurt us as much as or more than it does the person on whom it is poured.

4. The gain factor. Jesus talked about the dire consequences of those who come to the temple to worship and present their offerings and then remember that there is a problem between them and others (Matthew 5:21-23). The Lord says to *leave your offering there before the altar and go; first be reconciled to your brother, and then come and present your offering* (Matthew 5:24). If there is someone with whom we need to make things right, then we must go and be reconciled to that person before we give our offering. Jesus said, *If your brother sins, go and show him his* *fault in private; if he listens to you, you have won your brother* (Matthew 18:15).

A brother is a precious and terrible thing to waste. When we forgive, we heal a broken relationship and gain back a brother; but if we hold grudges and harbor bitterness and unforgiveness in our hearts, we disgrace God as children do when they fuss and fight and disgrace their parents.

An unforgiving spirit, rancor, division, and hostility drive away the lost. It delights the devil when we fail to forgive.

Those who have ever been in a church fight know that unforgiveness discourages the saints. The devil would rather start a church fuss than sell a barrel of whiskey. An unforgiving spirit, rancor, division, and hostility drive away the lost. It delights the devil when we fail to forgive.

I have invested my life in seeking to see lost people reconciled to God and for the Church to build bridges instead of fences between its leaders. We so often want to be forgiven before the Lord but forget that real forgiveness is demonstrated by how we treat our brothers and sisters.

Real revival is not just getting the roof off and getting right with God; real revival is getting the walls down and getting right with one another. In 2002, Dr. Bill Bright and I wrote a book entitled, *Beyond All Limits: The Synergistic Church for a Planet in Crisis*. In the book, Dr. Bright shared a story about a mighty revival in Africa that had an emphasis on *no roof and no walls*. The people in that revival did not want anything to separate them from God and the world.

The Costly Requirements for Forgiveness

Be kind to one another, tender-hearted, forgiving each other, just as God in Christ also has forgiven you (Ephesians 4:32). Jesus is the model of our forgiveness since He paid the price of redemption through His blood. We must also have a personal Gethsemane and Calvary if we are to truly forgive someone who has deeply hurt us.

1. Forgive freely. The Lord's forgiveness is free, spontaneous, and quick. We should not wait to forgive them until after we have exacted our revenge. Instead, we should be so anxious to forgive that we chase them down in order to forgive them. That is what God did for us. We love Him because He first loved us.

When Adam and Eve sinned against God in the Garden of Eden, God did not say, "Well, I'm going to wait; and if they come to me, I might be persuaded to forgive them." No, the Lord God came to the Garden and *called to the man, and said to him, "Where are you?"* (Genesis 3:9). That was not the voice of a detective but the voice of a broken-hearted God who was seeking someone who had sinned against Him, freely seeking to forgive. *If your brother sins, go and show him his fault in private* [it does not say to go and tell him off but to tell him secretly, privately, lovingly]; *if he listens to you, you have won your brother* (Matthew 18:15).

Then Peter came and said to Him, "Lord, how often shall my brother sin against me and I forgive him? Up to seven times?" [that's a perfect number] (Matthew 18:21). *Jesus said to him, "I do not say to you, up to seven times, but up to seventy times seven* — 490 times (Matthew 18:22). By inference, Jesus did not mean to stop at 491 times but was telling Peter to "get the mathematics out of it. Don't keep score. Forgiveness has no limit. Forget the math." To forgive freely even if we have to chase somebody down in order to forgive them.

2. **Forgive fully.** If someone says, "I want you to forgive me," we should not say, "Don't worry about it." That is a wrong response. We are to say, "I forgive you." This is very important because when we do wrong, we usually do not go to another individual and say, "Forgive me." Instead, we say, "If I have hurt your feelings, I'm sorry. I want to apologize."

If we have wronged someone, we are not to apologize but to seek their forgiveness.

The word *apologize* comes from the Greek word, *apologia*, which means "to make a defense." In apologetics, we are defending the faith so when we apologize, we are really defending ourselves. If we have wronged someone, we are not to apologize but to seek their forgiveness.

3. **Forgive finally.** We should not bring it up again. *I, even I, am the one who wipes out your transgressions for My own sake, And I will not remember your sins* (Isaiah 43:25). The sins are buried in the sea of God's forgetfulness. When we forgive, we must do it once and for all.

We may think, "Well, that brings up a problem for me. God doesn't remember our sins anymore? I thought God was omniscient. How can God ever truly forget anything?" Intellectually, God cannot forget; He does not lose His memory. When God says, *I will not remember your sins*, that means, "I will not bring them up. I will not use them against you. If I remember them, I remember them as forgiven sins. I don't continue to have that spirit of resentment that human beings tend to have. The sin is buried." Unfortunately, many times when we say we have forgiven, we have not forgiven finally.

The way we treat our brother and sister is a measurement of how much we truly love our heavenly Father.

---

4. Forgive forcefully. It is not natural to forgive. Our spirits demand justice. "They need to pay. They hurt us, and they need to understand just how badly they hurt us." In 1711, Alexander Pope, an English poet, said, "To err is human; to forgive, divine." We need Jesus to be forgiven and Jesus in order to forgive. *Be kind to one another, tenderhearted, forgiving each other, just as God in Christ also has forgiven you* (Ephesians 4:32). That kindness and tenderheartedness come from Jesus. The same one who has forgiven us is the one who puts His Spirit in us and enables us to have the strength and the power to forgive.

The Certain Results of Forgiveness

1. Personal emancipation. When there is forgiveness, there is personal emancipation. We are set free!

2. Mutual reconciliation. When there is forgiveness, there may be reconciliation between us and others. We will gain our brother and sister and set them free.

3. Spiritual rejuvenation. When there is forgiveness, there will be revival. As mentioned previously, real revival is not just getting the roof off and getting right with God, but it is getting the walls down and getting right with one another.

Christian leaders often preach forgiveness throughout the earth but find it difficult to forgive one another or partner with one another. The way we treat our brother and sister is a measurement of how much we truly love our heavenly Father. While we strive to win the world, let us be sure to keep our relationships with our brothers and sisters fresh and forgiven.

11

Our Watch in Christ

Each year many of us watch the college bowl games. One of the most memorable took place on January 1, 1929, at the Rose Bowl in Pasadena, California. The University of California Berkeley was playing Georgia Tech, and both schools were undefeated at that time.

It was late in the second quarter, and Georgia Tech had the ball. They were pressing hard on the 33-yard line when Stumpy Thomason was hit. Roy Riegels, University of California Berkeley's center, scooped up the ball, spun around, and headed toward the goal with the crowd cheering. With his eyes moving to the right and to the left, knees up high, and legs spread apart, he was running brilliantly. However, there was one "small" problem—he had somehow become confused and was literally headed for the wrong goal line with this scooped-up fumble.

Teammate and quarterback Benny Lom chased Riegels, screaming at him to stop. Known for his speed, Lom finally caught up with Riegels at California's 3-yard line and tried to turn him around, but he was immediately hit by Georgia Tech players and tackled back to the 1-yard line.

Imagine the shame and humiliation Riegels felt as he walked back to the bench — the jeers, the catcalls, the hooting. During the halftime exchange, Riegels said, "Coach, I can't do it. I've ruined you, I've ruined myself, I've ruined the University of California. I couldn't face that crowd to save my life." Head coach Nibs Price put his arm on Riegels' shoulder and spoke words of admonition and encouragement telling him to "Get up and go back out there — the game is only half over." They went into the second half, and Riegels played brilliantly.

Not only is this story one of the great epochs in football history, but it is also a parable of so many of us who think we are doing well in our business and relationships. There is one problem though — we are headed towards the wrong goal. The problem is that we have lost sight of the right goal, and it seems that Satan is leading interference for us.

I want to do the same thing for you that Benny Lom did for Roy Riegels: I want to try to tackle you and help you find God's goal for your life, live life to its fullest, and be all that you can be.

> *But all things become visible when they are exposed by the light, for everything that becomes visible is light. For this reason it says, "Awake, sleeper, And arise from the dead, And Christ will shine on you." Therefore be careful how you walk, not as unwise men but as wise, making the most of your time, because the days are evil. So then do not be foolish, but understand what the will of the Lord is. And do not get drunk with wine, for that*

is dissipation, but be filled with the Spirit (Ephesians 5:13-18).

There are two words that are translated as *time*. One is *chronos* from which we get *chronology* as in *making the most of your time* (Ephesians 5:16). It simply means "the passing of time," such as in so many hours, minutes, and seconds. Some people call their watches a *chronometer*—it just keeps count of the segments of time as it passes.

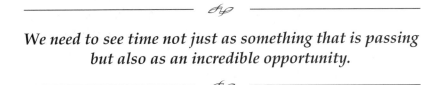

We need to see time not just as something that is passing but also as an incredible opportunity.

The other word that is translated as time is *kairos* which is more like "seasons of time" or literally "opportunity." *So then, while we have opportunity, let us do good to all people, and especially to those who are of the household of the faith* (Galatians 6:10).

When Ephesians 5:16 speaks of *making the most of your time*, it speaks of the hours, the minutes, and the seconds; but more than that, it really speaks of the opportunities we have. We need to see time not just as something that is passing but also as an incredible opportunity. Consequently, when we are making the most of our time, we are also making the most of our opportunities.

The days are evil (Ephesians 5:16), but we are to be buying up the opportunities. We are to live in wise ways for evil days; and because the days are evil, we must take advantage of every opportunity God gives us. If we are going toward the wrong goal or sitting on the sidelines, God's Word shows us how to take, use, and maximize our time for God's glory.

Time Is a Provided Opportunity

For this reason it says, "Awake, sleeper" (Ephesians 5:14). There is a day of opportunity that we dare not let pass by. Some have been chloroformed by these evil days and need to be jolted from their stupor.

Just as we need an alarm clock to get us up in the mornings, we also need the Lord to awaken us to the opportunities He has provided. It is God who is the creator of time, and His two greatest gifts to us are Jesus and time. God has given us time to work, serve, love, laugh, and labor; but like any gift, how we use it is really up to us. We need to see every day as a gift from God.

The LORD's loving kindnesses indeed never cease, for His compassions never fail (Lamentations 3:22). Time is something that God gives us today and will give us tomorrow; it is not something we own for God is the possessor of time. We are only stewards of the time and must eventually answer to God for what we did with every day He gave us. Twenty-four hours in a day, 1,440 minutes in a day, 86,000 seconds in a day — and every one of them is a precious gift from God.

Dr. Benjamin E. Mays wrote a poem that is very meaningful to me:

> I have only just a minute,
> Only sixty seconds in it.
> Forced upon me, can't refuse it.
> Didn't seek it, didn't choose it.
> But it's up to me to use it.
> I must suffer if I lose it.
> Give account if I abuse it.
> Just a tiny little minute,
> but eternity is in it.

We all have the same amount of time—24 hours in a day. The difference between people is not that some have more time than others but how people use the time that God has given them.

The difference between people is not that some have more time than others but how people use the time that God has given them.

Time Is a Present Opportunity

Therefore be careful how you walk, not as unwise men but as wise (Ephesians 5:15). *This is the day which the Lord has made; Let us rejoice and be glad in it* (Psalm 118:24). There are two days that can steal the joy and productivity from today: yesterday and tomorrow.

We are challenged to let go of yesterday. *I do not regard myself as having laid hold of it yet* [he did not think he had arrived nor that he was perfect]; *but one thing* I do [Paul was not a man of many ambitions he narrowed everything to one focus]: *forgetting what* lies *behind and reaching forward to what* lies *ahead, I press on toward the goal for the prize of the upward call of God in Christ Jesus* (Philippians 3:13-14).

Paul Had to Forget the Past

Forgetting what lies *behind* (Ephesians 3:13). Following are some of the things the Apostle Paul had to forget:

1. **He had to forget past guilt.** Along with others, the Apostle Paul was one who was guilty of the stoning of Stephen, but he buried that guilt in the

sea of God's forgetfulness. *Christ Jesus came into the world to save sinners, among whom I am foremost* of all (1 Timothy 1:15).
2. **He had to forget past glory.** Not only was Paul guilty of murder, but in the Christian Church he is also remembered as one of the greatest Christians, one of the greatest missionaries, and one of the greatest church planters the world has ever seen. In his day, he was not sitting around and considering his past or his future but was busy about the Lord's work daily.
3. **He had to forget past grief.** Paul suffered as few men ever have, but he referred to it as a *momentary, light affliction* (2 Corinthians 4:17). He felt that *the sufferings of this present time are not worthy to be compared with the glory that is to be revealed to us* (Romans 8:18) and said *one thing* I do: *forgetting what* lies behind and reaching forward to what lies ahead (Philippians 3:13).
4. **He had to forget past grudges.** There were many people who did Paul wrong. He was abused, lied about, mistreated, cheated, and overlooked; but he refused to feed a fever and nurse a grudge. He said, "I take my past guilt, I take my past glory, I take my past grief, I take my past grudges, and I forget those things which are behind."

Paul Was Not to Worry About Tomorrow

One thing that can take the joy out of today is yesterday if you carry the load from yesterday into today. Tomorrow can also take the joy out of today because tomorrow never comes. We are always looking forward to what is going to happen. We want friends so we look forward to having friends; and when we make friends, we weep when we lose them. Many times, we fail to enjoy friends while we have them.

Some people are waiting for tomorrow, and others are worrying about tomorrow. Jesus told us, *Do not worry about tomorrow; for tomorrow will care for itself. Each day has enough trouble of its own* (Matthew 6:34). In the crucible of His wisdom and the ecology of His grace, God allows trouble in our lives. The trouble is like an evil smell—something bad. We all have difficulties, but we all need difficulties. We are blessed with difficulties for God allows them to cause us to come to Him.

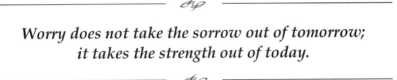

Worry does not take the sorrow out of tomorrow; it takes the strength out of today.

The worst thing that could happen to us would be not to have any difficulties because then we would never know our need of the Lord. God gives us enough difficulties to bring us to Him but also gives us enough grace to meet those difficulties. There is a perfect balance of difficulties and grace.

When we worry, we reach into tomorrow and take tomorrow's difficulty and bring it into today. God does not give grace for tomorrow's difficulty for *tomorrow will care for itself. Each day has enough trouble of its own* (Matthew 6:34). *According to your days, so will your leisurely walk be* (Deuteronomy 33:25).

When we reach into tomorrow and bring tomorrow's troubles—real or imaginary—into today, we overload the circuit and upset God's divine ecology. Worry does not take the sorrow out of tomorrow; it takes the strength out of today. Then when we meet tomorrow, we meet it out of breath because we are already on overload from today.

Sanskrit literature tells us to:

Look well to this one day, for it and it alone is life. In the brief course of this day lie all the verities and realities of your existence; the pride of growth, the glory of action, the splendor of beauty. Yesterday is only a dream, and tomorrow is but a vision. Yet each day, well lived, makes every yesterday a dream of happiness and each tomorrow, a vision of hope. Look well, therefore, to this one day, for it and it alone is life.

Time Is a Precious Opportunity

Paul tells us to be *making the most of* [our] *time* (Ephesians 5:16) or as the King James Version puts it, *redeeming the time*. When we redeem something, we pay for it. There is something we must give in exchange if we want to live up to the opportunities God gives us. We must realize how valuable time is. To waste time is to waste life because time is the stuff life is made of. A person who is killing time is not killing time but themselves—committing suicide by degrees.

In the true sense, a murderer does not take someone's life because that person is going to die anyway. What the murderer does is take that person's time by causing that person to die sooner. Time is life, and it is precious. When we give someone our time, we are giving a piece of ourselves—something even heaven cannot give for in heaven there is no time. However, time on earth is so valuable and important that we must redeem it.

Ephesians 5:15 tell us to walk *not as unwise men but as wise*. Wisdom is the art of spending time prudently *so teach us to number our days, that we may present to You a heart of wisdom* (Psalm 90:12).

There are several ways we can redeem the time.

1. The Prayer Principle. It is very important that we begin our day with prayer for prayer is the key that unlocks the door of the morning. The poet Thomas Blake said, "Every morning lean your arms awhile upon the windowsill of heaven and gaze upon the Lord. Then with the vision in your heart, turn strong to meet your day."

As you greet the day, spend enough time in prayer to receive God's will for your life for that day. It is no more a waste of time to wait on God in the morning than for a woodchopper to waste time when sharpening his axe.

It is an insult to God to say we do not have enough time. If we do not have enough time, we are doing something God did not intend for us to do—either something we have imposed upon ourselves or something we have allowed others to impose upon us. The purpose of prayer every morning—the principle of prayer—is to get quiet before the Lord and let God speak to our hearts.

2. The Priority Principle. After God speaks to us, it is very obvious that we have been given priorities. Life would be simple if it were a choice between good and bad; however, most of the choices we have to make are between good and best. We need to find out what God wants us to do.

Most of the time, management books tell us how to get more things done, but what we do is far more important than *how* we do it.

We must get our priorities right. Jesus lived only to the age of 33 in His humanity on earth; but when He bowed His head on the cross, He said, *It is finished!* (John 19:30). He had told the Father, *I glorified You on the earth, having accomplished the work which You have given Me to do* (John 17:4).

There were many villages wanting Jesus to come and teach and many places wanting Jesus to come and heal, but Jesus did not do everything or go everywhere. When the crowds were clamoring after Jesus, He sometimes withdrew to be alone; but He could say at the end of His ministry, *I glorified You on the earth, having accomplished the work which You have given Me to do* (John 17:4).

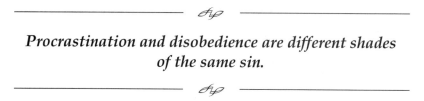

Procrastination and disobedience are different shades of the same sin.

3. The Promptness Principle. This deals with the sin of procrastination. *Therefore, to one who knows the right thing to do and does not do it, to him it is sin* (James 4:17). Sin is not just merely doing wrong; it is failing to do what we ought to do. Procrastination and disobedience are different shades of the same sin, and we should desire to cultivate the habit of instant obedience.

Most people fail in the area of willpower, a good definition of which is: "When you have a job to do, begin this very hour. You supply the will, and God supplies the power." When there is something you know you ought to do, do it, and do it now.

4. The Power Principle. *Making the most of your time* (Ephesians 5:16). That is the promptness principle. *Do not be foolish, but understand what the will of the Lord is* (Ephesians 5:17). That is the prayer principle. *And do not get drunk with wine, for that is dissipation, but be filled with the Spirit* (Ephesians 5:18). That is the power principle.

The power principle is to do God's will in the power of the Holy Spirit. Most of us do not need to learn to work harder; we need to learn to work with more power and effectiveness.

Time Is a Passing Opportunity

The days are evil. Time is passing away. This day is passing away, and we must give an account for it. Time is such a strange commodity for we cannot save it, borrow it, loan it, leave it, take it, or give it. All we can do is use it or lose it.

I would to God that we would all live in the eternal now and cut ourselves loose from yesterday.

Time cannot be stopped. In a football game, a *time-out* can be called but not in life. Time cannot be stored. We can put our money in a bank but not our time. Time cannot be stretched. We can add another cup of water to the soup to stretch it, but there is no way to stretch time. Time cannot be shared. We can share our books, our money, and our automobiles, but we cannot share our time. We can give a part of our time to others; but when we share our time in that sense, we still have not added any time to their lives.

Time is a passing opportunity. What do we intend to do? Be a soul winner? When? Be a good steward? When? Make reconciliation with an estranged friend? When? Call our mother? When? Write a letter to our dad and tell him how much we love him and thank God for the sacrifices he made for so many years? When? Time cannot be stopped, it cannot be stored, it cannot be saved, it cannot be shared.

Therefore be careful how you walk, not as unwise men but as wise, making the most of your time, because the days are evil (Ephesians 5:15-16).

> *Lost — yesterday, somewhere between sunrise and sunset, two golden hours, each set with sixty diamond minutes. No reward is offered, for they are gone forever* (Horace Mann).

I would to God that we would all live in the eternal now and cut ourselves loose from yesterday. Last year, with its heartaches and failures gone. Forget those things that are behind, confess them to the Lord, and bury them in the sea of God's forgetfulness. Tomorrow is a time nowhere but on a fool's calendar. Stop saying, "If I had the time." We do have the time; use it.

Our Will in Christ

So then do not be foolish, but understand what the will of the Lord is (Ephesians 5:17).

We are living in perilous times with many problems confronting us. We are facing the threatening clouds of war in the Middle East and a world in which morals are declining at an alarming and increasing rate. We are facing school systems that are infiltrated and injected with atheism.

We are facing countless pulpits with contaminated ministers who no longer believe the miraculous in Scripture. Church rolls are filled with those who have never repented of their sins. We see a world in need where the play palaces and the temples of sin are crowded with people while many churches cannot even muster a respectable crowd on Sunday nights. For the most part, the American Church has decided that Sunday night services are a "thing of the past" and have canceled them rather than reflecting on the lack of thirst the "saints" have to be in the House of God while preferring to sit in front of a television. Church rolls are padded, but pews are empty. We see a world that is being baptized in tears while very few souls are being baptized in water. The sad part of it is that while the world has forgotten to blush, the church has forgotten to weep.

While the world has forgotten to blush, the church has forgotten to weep.

If that were not enough, we are confronted with COVID-19 which spread worldwide in less than three months. We should be safe but sensible, factual but not fearful, wise but not worried, informed but inspired, and clean but confident!

What Is the Answer?

What can be done about threatening war? What can be done about declining morals? What can be done about corruption in education, politics, and religion? What can be done about people's indifference? What will it take to turn our cities around? What will it take to turn our nation around? What will it take to bless our world? What should be our response to COVID-19?

We are facing one of three things: revival, ruin, or Jesus' return. May it be a spiritual revival that will be the return of the Lord Jesus Christ!

However, if it is a spiritual revival, how will it come about? *So then do not be foolish, but understand what the will of the Lord is* (Ephesians 5:17). What is the will of the Lord? *Do not get drunk with wine, for that is dissipation, but be filled with the Spirit* (Ephesians 5:18). The will of the Lord is that the Church of the living God *be filled with the Spirit* of the living God—this alone is the answer!

1. Education is not the answer. People have tried everything. Some denominations believe that the answer is the intellect and spend millions of dollars on teaching programs. Students go to class after class with their heads growing full while their hearts remain empty. Mahatma Gandhi's son said, "In India, the missionaries taught our people how to read; and the communists are now giving them the material to read." Education is not the answer.

2. Activism is not the answer. The activists in the Church say, "We'd all better get busy. We've got to work harder—work, work, work. You know, get busy, try harder; a busy Christian is a happy Christian so get with it."

Consequently, they work and they work and they work without finding answers. We might as well tell a sick man to get out of his bed and do the work of a well man as to tell the Church of the living God that what she needs to do is get busy.

3. Emotionalism is not the answer. The emotionalist says, "I have the answer. We need to get everyone all stirred up with rhythm, music, cheerleader-type enthusiasm, crocodile tears, and all of these kinds of things."

We try to tell people that if they can just get that certain feeling, everything will be fine. So a man gets himself psyched up to a certain emotional level; but when he goes home, he loses the enthusiasm of the moment leaving him with only the memory of an emotion. His latter state is worse than his first because he is now depressed and says, "I had it, but I lost it."

There is nothing wrong with activity. There is nothing wrong with study. There is nothing wrong with emotion; however, they are not the answer.

4. Pharisaism is not the answer. The "Pharisees" in the church say, "The church is not separated enough, and we need to stop doing this, and stop doing that, and stop doing the other."

The emphasis is on the words **be** *filled, not* **get** *filled.*

God knows there are things we ought to stop doing, but the "Pharisees" have a negative religion that is rooted in giving things up. While limbs are pruned and roots are strengthened, the "Pharisee" becomes hard and bitter.

A Spirit-filled Church Is the Answer

There is only one answer for the needs of our world, and that is a Spirit-filled church. *Understand what the will of the Lord is. And do not get drunk with wine . . . but be filled with the Spirit* (Ephesians 5:17-18).

What Does It Mean to Be Filled with the Spirit?

1. Continuous control by the Spirit. The hope of this world is for the Christian to be in the continuous control of the Holy Spirit. The emphasis is on the words *be* filled, not *get* filled. The Bible does not say to *get* filled with the

Spirit but to *be* filled with the Spirit (Ephesians 5:18). The word implies a continuous control by the Holy Spirit.

Which is the most important question: "*Were* you married?" or "*Are* you married?" The fact that you *got* married does not necessarily mean that you *are* married. The fact that you *were* filled with the Spirit does not necessarily mean that you *are* filled with the Spirit.

Being filled with the Spirit is not a crisis experience. There was a time when we were *not* filled with the Spirit, but we *got* filled with the Spirit. God's emphasis is not on *getting* filled but upon the day-by-day experience of *being* filled. Yesterday's experience is not good for today.

The Bible implies a continual control by the Holy Spirit—not *getting* filled but *being* filled. At this very moment, are you filled with the Holy Spirit? I am not talking about your experience in the past but your present experience of being filled with the Holy Spirit. If there was ever a time in your life when you were closer to God than you are at this moment, then you are a backslider. *Be filled* (Ephesians 5:18).

To be filled with the Spirit means a continual, moment-by-moment, day-by-day-by-day experience of being filled with the Spirit. How does a man get drunk? He drinks. How does he stay drunk? He keeps drinking. *Do not get drunk with wine, for that is dissipation, but be filled with the Spirit* (Ephesians 5:18) is literally what the Greek says. *Be filled with the Spirit* day-by-day, moment-by-moment.

2. Subjection to the Spirit. We are to be subject to the Spirit. The Holy Spirit is not a substance; the Holy Spirit is a person. When the Bible uses the term *being filled with the Spirit*, it is speaking in the terminology of our bodies as being temples and the Holy Spirit as a person possessing every room and the key to every door.

A lot of people talk about getting the Holy Spirit and wanting more of the Holy Spirit. The problem is not for us to get more of the Holy Spirit for *He gives the Spirit without measure* (John 3:34). We have all of the Holy Spirit we are ever going to get. You cannot have just a part of the Holy Spirit. He did not say, "I'll give you a third of the Holy Spirit." He does not give the Spirit by measure. It is not getting more of the Spirit but letting the Holy Spirit have full control in our lives. It is turning everything over to the Holy Spirit.

While the Holy Spirit comes to abide in every person, He does not preside in every person.

When we get saved, we have Him in us; but when we are filled with the Spirit, He has us—all of us. When a person gets saved, the Holy Spirit comes in and abides; and if that person does not have the Holy Spirit within, they are not saved. *If anyone does not have the Spirit of Christ, he does not belong to Him* (Romans 8:9). After that, we are saved and sealed with the Holy Spirit of promise. God sends forth His Spirit into our hearts *crying, "Abba! Father!"* (Galatians 4:6). That is one way we know we are saved—because of the witness of the Spirit within us.

However, while the Holy Spirit comes to abide in every person, He does not preside in every person. While everyone has Him as a resident, not everyone has Him as a president. The idea though is to let Him be president—to let Him take over completely. It is not like filling a bottle with a substance but more like turning the keys to a house over to someone.

We are to be in subjection to the Spirit; however, most of us want the Holy Spirit to be in subjection to us.

When we choose to move in the Spirit, we will have to face battles. When the Israelites came out of Egypt and walked through the wilderness and into Canaan, that is a picture of an unsaved person coming out of the world of sin, through the wilderness of carnality, and into the blessings of the deeper, Spirit-filled life. Egypt is a picture of the world, the wilderness is a picture of the carnal Christian, and Canaan is a picture of the Spirit-filled life.

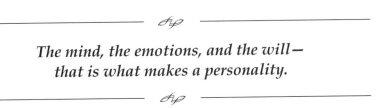

The mind, the emotions, and the will— that is what makes a personality.

It was not until the Israelites got into Canaan that they really became involved in warfare. They only had a few skirmishes in the wilderness. The carnal Christian does not have as many battles with the devil as the Spirit-filled Christian. It was after Jesus was anointed with the Holy Spirit at His baptism that He met Satan head-on. When God opens the windows of heaven to bless us, the devil opens the doors of hell to blast us. When the Israelites got to Canaan, it was there that they came into conflict with the Canaanite worshippers of demons.

3. Possession by a Person. To be filled with the Spirit not only means there must be continuous control by the Spirit and subjection to the Spirit, but also there must be possession by the person of the Holy Spirit. *Do not get drunk with wine . . . but be filled with the Spirit* (Ephesians 5:18).

Notice carefully — not be filled *by* the Spirit but be filled *with* the Spirit. Do not get the idea that the Spirit is standing beside you filling you with love, with power, with peace, with understanding, with wisdom, or with all you need. The emphasis is not on *getting* filled by the Spirit but on *being* filled with the Spirit. It is not an influence, a force, or a power but rather another person taking control.

The Holy Spirit Has a Mind

One of the marks of personality is intelligence. *He who searches the hearts knows what the mind of the Spirit is, because He intercedes for the saints according to* the will *of God* (Romans 8:27). The Holy Spirit is a person of intelligence.

Though the magistrates commanded Peter and John not to speak anymore in the name of Jesus, *they observed the confidence of Peter and John and understood that they were uneducated and untrained men, they were amazed, and began to recognize them as having been with Jesus* (Acts 4:13). They spoke like Jesus of whom had been said, *Never has a man spoken the way this man speaks* (John 7:46). Where did these ignorant fishermen get that knowledge? From the Holy Spirit.

The Holy Spirit Has Emotions

> *Now I urge you, brethren, by our Lord Jesus Christ and by the love of the Spirit, to strive together with me in your prayers to God for me* [the love of the Spirit] (Romans 15:30). *Do not grieve the Holy Spirit of God, by whom you were sealed for the day of redemption* (Ephesians 4:30).

The Holy Spirit Has a Will

While they were ministering to the Lord and fasting, the Holy Spirit said, "Set apart for Me Barnabas and Saul for the work to which I have called them" (Acts 13:2). The Holy Spirit gives spiritual gifts to every man *individually just as He wills* (1 Corinthians 12:11).

When we are filled with the Spirit of God, all the fullness of the Godhead dwells in Jesus; and Jesus dwells in us through His Holy Spirit.

The mind, the emotions, and the will—that is what makes a personality. The Holy Spirit does not have a body nor does God the Father; yet God the Father is mind, emotion, and will—a person.

When the Bible says we are to be filled with the Holy Spirit, it is not that we are to be filled *by* the Holy Spirit but *with* the Holy Spirit. As a person, the Holy Spirit comes into us. What difference does it make whether we are filled *by* the Spirit or *with* the Spirit? If we are filled *by* the Spirit and the Spirit gives us love when we need patience, then we are lacking what we need.

If He gives us patience when we need wisdom, then we are lacking again. However, if we are filled with a person and that person has everything we need, then we will not be lacking anything at all! When we are filled with the Spirit of God, all the fullness of the Godhead dwells in Jesus; and Jesus dwells in us through His Holy Spirit.

The need of the Church is to understand what the will of God is and to be filled with the Spirit—not *get* filled but *be* filled; not have Him but let Him have you; not get a substance but let a person come in, move you off the throne, and take over.

We have come back to the beginning. COVID-19 spread worldwide in less than three months. We should be safe but sensible, factual but not fearful, wise but not worried, informed but inspired, and clean but confident. The will of God in times like these is to be filled with the Spirit!

Our Wedding in Christ

Everyone does not have to get married nor is it God's plan for everyone to be married. God talks about the sanctity of the single life just as He talks about the marvels and the wonders of married life.

In his book, *Brave New World*, Aldous Huxley suggested that marriage licenses may one day be sold like dog licenses—good for twelve months with no law against changing dogs or keeping more than one animal at a time. Without divine intervention and some common sense, this is the kind of world into which we are moving.

Jeremy Taylor said, "A good mate is heaven's last and best gift to man: her voice his sweetest music, her smile his brightest day, her lips his faithful counselor, and her prayers the ablest advocate of heaven's blessings on his head."

The Holy Spirit inspired the Apostle Paul's words as he gave instructions to husbands: *Husbands, love your wives, just as Christ also loved the church and gave Himself up for her* (Ephesians 5:25). Paul uses this object lesson to teach us the qualities of a Spirit-filled husband.

The Position of a Spirit-filled Husband

The husband has the position of headship. *Wives, be subject to your own husbands, as to the Lord. For the husband is the head of the wife, as Christ also is the head of the church* (Ephesians 5:22-23).

Husbands are not to be bosses, dictators, or tyrants but are to lead their wives lovingly as Christ leads the Church.

Paul also tells us that a woman is to submit to her husband which is diametrically opposed to the ways of the world because the world tells wives stand up for their rights and not to submit to anyone for any reason. However, the husband is the biblical head of the wife that there might be a chain of command that would link a home to heaven and authority in the home.

God wants the home to have a head because anything without a head is dead and anything with two heads is a freak. This does not mean that the husband is better than the wife nor that submission means inferiority. *But I want you to understand that Christ is the head of every man, and the man is the head of a woman, and God is the head of Christ* (1 Corinthians 11:3). This verse states clearly and plainly that

God has a chain of command: God the father, God the son, man, and woman.

Many have concluded that if the woman is under the man, the woman is inferior to the man. Christ is under the Father, but that does not mean that the Son is inferior to the Father. We serve one God in three persons: God the Father, God the Son, and God the Holy Spirit who are coequal and co-eternal. *Let this mind be in you, which was also in Christ Jesus: Who, being in the form of God, thought it not robbery to be equal with God: But made himself of no reputation, and took upon him the form of a servant* (Philippians 2:5-7 KJV). Jesus submitted willingly.

Husbands are not to be bosses, dictators, or tyrants but are to lead their wives lovingly as Christ leads the Church.

The Pattern of a Spirit-filled Husband

For the husband is the head of the wife, as Christ also is the head of the church (Ephesians 5:23).

Jesus has committed the evangelization of the world to the Church. In the same way, a husband can depend and lean upon his wife, and his wife can have great responsibilities. A woman is often more gifted in finances, in planning, or in business than a man.

This does not mean that because he is the head that he is not going to depend upon her or let her give insight or wisdom in these areas. If she has strength in a particular area, the husband ought to depend upon her. He is to love his wife as Christ loved the Church. The pattern for the husband is Christ.

The position of a Spirit-filled husband is the head; the pattern of the Spirit-filled husband is the Lord Jesus Christ; and Jesus is the example for the way a husband is to love his wife.

The Practice of a Spirit-filled Husband

Husbands, love your wives (Ephesians 5:25). This is a command from God; and anything God commands husbands to do, He also enables them to do. However, this love is a Christlike love, not a romantic love.

1. Husbands are to love their wives **selflessly**. *Husbands, love your wives, just as Christ also loved the church and gave Himself up for her* (Ephesians 5:25). Husbands can no longer make decisions on the basis of just what they want to do but must live selflessly, taking the wife into consideration in every decision.

2. Husbands are to love their wives **sacrificially**. *Christ gave Himself up for her* (Ephesians 5:25). Christ died for the Church, and a man must die to his singleness when he marries. In addition to a wedding, most marriages in America also need two funerals where the husband and wife both say, "I'm going to die to the old way — to singleness," after which they come together in one unique, new relationship. Since husbands must love their wives sacrificially, there is nothing too precious to give up for her — the hunting trip, fishing trip, or golf game.

3. Husbands must love their wives **sanctifyingly**. *That he might sanctify and cleanse it with the washing of water by the word, that he might present it to himself a glorious church, not having spot, or wrinkle, or any such thing; but that it should be holy and without blemish. So ought men to love their wives as their own bodies* (Ephesians 5:26-28 KJV).

For men to love their wives sanctifyingly means they are to be the spiritual leader in the home for God demands holiness, spirituality, and purity in husbands. In addition, husbands are to be prophets and priests in their homes and lead their wives.

The duty of a husband is to make his wife a radiantly beautiful Christian. Jesus is doing this with the Church *that he might sanctify and cleanse it with the washing of water by the word, That he might present it to himself a glorious church, not having spot, or wrinkle, or any such thing* (Ephesians 5-26-27 KJV). Husbands are to accomplish this by interceding for, leading, teaching, and protecting their wives spiritually.

In order for a husband to satisfy his wife, he must know what her needs are; and in order to know what her needs are, he must listen.

---

4. Husbands must love their wives **satisfyingly**. *So husbands ought also to love their own wives as their own bodies. He who loves his own wife loves himself; for no one ever hated his own flesh* (Ephesians 5:28-29).

We may hate the way a part of our body looks and think, "Boy, I wish it were stronger or better"; but when a part of our body is hurt or injured, we quickly seek medical assistance. When we are thirsty, we get a drink of water; when we are hungry, we eat; and when our bodies are tired, we rest. When our bodies have a need—whatever that need is—we want it satisfied and satisfied as quickly as is possible.

Men are to love their wives as Christ loved the Church and then love them as they love their own bodies, seeing that their wives' needs are met just as they see that the needs of their own bodies are met.

Unfortunately, many husbands fail to see that their wives are indeed their body. *We are members of His body*

(Ephesians 5:30); and just as we are members of Jesus' body — His flesh and His bones — our wives are members of our flesh. *No one ever hated his own flesh* (Ephesians 5:29).

There is something wrong with a man who does not care what happens to his own body; consequently, if a husband does not care for his wife, that marriage is sick. A man should be good to himself and love his wife for when he does, he loves himself and every blessing she receives is his blessing and each need he meets for her is a need that is ultimately being met in his own heart.

In order for a husband to satisfy his wife, he must know what her needs are; and in order to know what her needs are, he must listen. Our bodies have a central nervous system with little censors that cry out and tell us when we are thirsty, hungry, need rest, etc. Men need to develop a spiritual sensitivity in order to hear, feel, and understand the needs of their wives in order to love them and love them satisfyingly.

5. Husbands are to love their wives **supremely**. We are members of His body. For this reason a man shall leave his father and mother and shall be joined to his wife, and the two shall become one flesh (Ephesians 5:30-31).

Of all human relationships, that of a husband and a wife is uniquely supreme. It is not said of any other relationship that they shall become one flesh. Therefore, the relationship of the husband to his wife and the wife to her husband is a deeper relationship, more supremely unique and different, than any other human relationship — far deeper than the relationship of two friends, two business partners, or a parent and a child.

When a man gets saved, he becomes one flesh with the Lord Jesus Christ; therefore, he is to love his wife supremely. There is a wonderful feeling that a woman has when she knows she is number one; there is no higher relationship. The best thing a husband can do for his children is to love their mother.

It does not make a wife feel insecure when her husband tells her, "I love you more than anything or anyone except Jesus Christ." This type of commitment to Christ makes her feel more secure. A man does not love his wife less when he loves God more. In actuality, he cannot really love his wife until he loves God as he ought.

There is no love greater than Christ's love for the Church and the love husbands are to have for their wives, and this is accomplished by being filled with the Spirit.

6. Husbands are to love their wives **steadfastly**. For this reason a man shall leave his father and mother and shall be joined to his wife, and the two shall become one flesh (Ephesians 5:31). Divorce is a tragedy of tragedies because God's plan is for one man to be married to one woman "'til death they do part."

> *For I am convinced that neither death, nor life, nor angels, nor principalities, nor things present, nor things to come, nor powers, nor height, nor depth, nor any other created thing, will be able to separate us from the love of God, which is in Christ Jesus our Lord* (Romans 8:38-39).

There is no love greater than Christ's love for the Church and the love husbands are to have for their wives, and this is accomplished by being filled with the Spirit: *Do not get drunk with wine, for that is dissipation, but be filled with the Spirit* (Ephesians 5:18).

Husbands cannot fulfill this kind of love to their wives in their own human strength nor can wives submit to their husbands in their own human strength. This type of love is the love of Jesus Christ in us. Men must love their wives with the love of Jesus; and in order to have that love of Jesus, they must first be saved and filled with the Spirit. There is no way to build a home except with the Lord. *Unless the Lord builds the house, they labor in vain who build it* (Psalm 127:1).

14

Our Way in Christ

Imagine a man who saved enough money to buy a brand-new automobile although he had never owned one before and had no understanding of it. He showed the car off to his friends—its beautiful paint job, the soft upholstery, the stereo with Sirius Xm—all the amenities.

However, there was one major thing he did NOT understand about the automobile—that it had an engine in it. Consequently, everywhere he went, he pushed the car except when he was going downhill and could get in and coast. Unfortunately though, that did not thrill him too much because he knew he was going to have to push it up the next hill. Over time, this automobile that was supposed to be a blessing to him became a burden to him. Rather than the car carrying him, he was pushing it. Even so, he was very proud of it and very grateful to have it— most of the time.

One day, someone showed him the ignition key and said, "Put that right in there and turn it." He turned it and heard a surge of power. "What's that?!" "The engine—the motor. Now put it in drive and push that pedal down." When he did, the car roared in a surge of power; and he said, "Why, this is wonderful! This is glorious! Why didn't someone tell me sooner?"

Being saved is not a matter of what you do for God but a matter of what God does through you by the fullness of the Holy Spirit.

Some might say, "That is a lame story; nobody could be that dumb." They would be correct—unless it is the Christian who does not understand the ministry of the Holy Spirit.

When God saved us, He gave us a faith with an engine in it. Unfortunately, there are many people who are still pushing their faith rather than letting their faith carry them; and the faith—the salvation—that was meant to be a blessing has almost become a burden. They are grateful to be saved but secretly think, "Being a Christian is SUCH a difficult thing!"

The ignition key to this thing called Christianity is *do not get drunk with wine, for that is dissipation, but be filled with the Spirit* (Ephesians 5:18).

There are some personal questions that are not polite to ask such as "How much money do you make?" or "How much did you pay for your house?" However, there are some personal questions that are vital questions to ask such as "Are you being filled with the Spirit right now?" not "Does the Holy Spirit indwell you?" because

He indwells all Christians and not "Do you believe in the fullness of the Spirit?" or even "Have you been filled with the Spirit?" The question is a very personal question: "Are you being filled with the Holy Spirit right now?"

Being saved is not a matter of what you do for God but a matter of what God does through you by the fullness of the Holy Spirit. *Be filled with the Spirit* (Ephesians 5:18).

We Need to Understand the Reasons for Being Spirit-filled

1. Our obedience. Ephesians 5:18 is not a suggestion nor a request but a command of God.

The words, *be filled* (Ephesians 5:18), are in what we call the *imperative mood* which expresses a command. If someone says, "It is imperative that you do this or that," they are not giving an option. The Christian who is not Spirit-filled is living in rebellion against God — present tense. That is the reason for the question, "Are you being filled with the Spirit right now?" not "Have you been filled with the Spirit?" *Be filled* — right now, present tense.

Furthermore, it is plural in number. The command is not just to the pastor, the minister of music, the soloist, or the missionary but also *the promise is for you and your children and for all who are far off, as many as the Lord our God will call* (Acts 2:39). Every boy and girl who knows Jesus ought to be Spirit-filled along with every evangelist and every layperson. *Be filled with the Spirit* (Ephesians 5:18) — all of us.

It is passive in voice. That means He is not saying, "Get filled" but *be filled* (Ephesians 5:18). It is not what we do but what He does in and through us.

Do not get drunk with wine . . . but be filled with the Spirit (Ephesians 5:18). We tend to camp on the first part of that verse, *Do not get drunk with wine,* while ignoring the second part of that verse, *but be filled with the Spirit.* While we are commanded not to get drunk with wine, it is a greater sin not to be filled with the Spirit.

We should be Spirit-filled because it is a command to obey as well as a blessing to enjoy.

Most who read this will disagree, but I believe it is a greater sin not to be filled with the Spirit than to be drunk with wine because the Bible teaches that the sins of omission are greater than the sins of commission. It is a greater sin to fail to do what you ought to do than to do what you ought not to do.

Why? Because if you are doing what you ought to do, you cannot be doing what you ought not do; but if you are doing what you ought not do, you will not be doing what you ought to do. The sin of omission is a greater sin than the sin of commission.

Though I put no premium on nor make light of getting drunk, I am saying that we should be Spirit-filled because it is a command to obey as well as a blessing to enjoy.

2. Our obligations. When we think about the obligations that are ours as Christians, we should think about what the Bible commands us to do and how we are going to do what the Bible commands us to do because in and of ourselves, we do not have the strength.

Our worship life. *Speaking to one another in psalms and hymns and spiritual songs, singing and making melody with your heart to the Lord; always giving thanks for all things in the name of our Lord Jesus Christ to God, even the Father*

(Ephesians 5:19-20). In our worship life, we need to be filled with the Holy Spirit because *God is spirit, and those who worship Him must worship in spirit and truth* (John 4:24).

We have all been to worship services where people are trying to worship God in the flesh—tedious, tasteless, and full of carnality. On the other hand, we have also been in worship services where those who are leading the worship are filled with God's blessed Holy Spirit and those in the congregation are singing praises to God and worshiping Him in Spirit and in truth. The only way to truly worship God is in the Spirit.

Our wedded life. *Wives, be subject to your own husbands, as to the Lord* (Ephesians 5:22). A wife is to respect, love, and submit to her husband as if he were Jesus Christ.

As mentioned previously, Paul does not mean that the wife is inferior to the husband. In actuality, many women are superior to their husbands; but men and women before the Lord are all equal. Nevertheless, the Bible still says that wives are to submit to their own husbands even though it is not in human nature to do that.

We may think that the Bible always gives the hard things to the women; however, Paul really gave the harder things to the men when he said, *Husbands, love your wives, just as Christ also loved the church and gave Himself up for her* (Ephesians 5:25). The wife is to submit to the husband as if the husband were Jesus Christ; and the husband is to love the wife as if he were Jesus Christ because Jesus loved the Church sacrificially and died for the Church. A husband ought to love his wife so much that he is willing to die for her and show it by the way he lives for her. Most women would not have any difficulty submitting to a husband who loved her enough to die for her and showed it by the way he lives for her.

Husbands, love your wives, just as Christ also loved the church (Ephesians 5:25). We can do nothing that Jesus did for we do not have the ability. The only way is for Jesus in us to do it.

We can do nothing that Jesus did for we do not have the ability. The only way is for Jesus in us to do it.

My wife, Sheri, does not mind being second in my life. When Jesus Christ is enthroned and I am Spirit-filled, I love her better than I could if she were number one in my life. When she is number two, she receives far more love than if she were number one because God is loving her.

Our work life. We need to be Spirit-filled in our work life. *Slaves, be obedient to those who are your masters according to the flesh, with fear and trembling, in the sincerity of your heart, as to Christ* (Ephesians 6:5).

We are to serve our boss as if we were serving Jesus Christ. We think, "I can't do it! He's not even a Christian! How can I serve him as if I were serving Jesus Christ?" *Not by way of eyeservice, as men-pleasers, but as slaves of Christ, doing the will of God from the heart. With good will render service, as to the Lord, and not to men* (Ephesians 6:6-7). We work for our boss as if we were working for Jesus Christ. When we go to work and walk through the door, we ought to have the same enthusiasm for the boss and the business as we have when we go to church. If Christians would begin to live like that on Monday, people would start believing what pastors preach on Sunday. They would more quickly believe the gospel. There is no better place to be a witness for Jesus Christ than on the job. Our job is our temple of devotion, our lamp stand for witness.

The boss would then say, "I don't understand these Christians. Why, they're here on time; they work with a smile on their face; they're very careful. They're honest and wouldn't steal a thing. I can trust them with the entire business because they seem to be as devoted to the business as if they own it."

When employers go to an employment agency to find workers, they ought to say, "By the way, if you have any Spirit-filled Christians, send them over. Those are the kind of people I want."

However, it is usually not human nature to work in such a manner. Human nature is for a person to get by with working as little as possible while earning as much as possible. John Wesley once said, "Get all you can, save all you can, give all you can." The equivalent of that philosophy in our culture seems to be, "Get all you can, can all you get [save], sit on the can [guard your gains so no one else shares them], and poison the rest." We live in a culture of greed, always wanting more.

Our war life. *Finally, be strong in the Lord and in the strength of His might. Put on the full armor of God* (Ephesians 6:10-11). This is in the context of being filled with the Spirit. We are in a battle with an enemy who is real, malevolent, cunning, sinister, and very active. He has marshaled all the forces of hell against us and our families. His desire is to sabotage our lives and bring devastation to our homes, our health and our happiness. We are no match for this enemy for he is stronger and more powerful; however, *greater is He who is in you than he who is in the world* (1 John 4:4). The only way we will win in this war is to be filled with the Holy Spirit of God.

Our witnessing life. *With all prayer and petition pray at all times in the Spirit, and with this in view, be on the alert with all perseverance and petition for all the saints, and pray on my behalf, that utterance may be given to me in the opening of my mouth, to make known with boldness the mystery of the gospel* (Ephesians 6:18-19).

We can preach truth, but only the Holy Spirit can impart truth.

How important it is that we be filled with the Spirit! We can preach truth, but only the Holy Spirit can impart truth; therefore, we are totally dependent upon the Holy Spirit. Whether we are witnessing on the street, in a business, in a classroom, in a home, or from the pulpit, we must be filled with the Spirit of God!

3. Our opportunities. *For this reason it says, "Awake, sleeper, And arise from the dead, And Christ will shine on you." Therefore be careful how you walk, not as unwise men but as wise* [if you are not Spirit-filled, you are not wise], *making the most of your time, because the days are evil. So then do not be foolish, but understand what the will of the Lord is. And do not get drunk with wine, for that is dissipation, but be filled with the Spirit* (Ephesians 5:14-18).

If the days were evil in Paul's day, how much more so is it in our day. We are up against the organized, mobilized, demonized forces of hell. Sometimes the battle comes as a frontal attack and at other times very subtly.

While we are in a war, there has never been a greater day, a greater age, or a greater opportunity to preach the gospel of Jesus Christ than right now. There is more hunger for the gospel and more openness to the gospel now than ever before. As the night grows darker, the saints grow brighter; and the hunger is more intense. People are looking, waiting, and wondering if they can find a way or if there is an answer; and we know the answer is in Christ.

---

*Christianity has not failed;
it just has not been tried in many places.*

We must not let this opportunity slip through our hands like sand falling to the ground. Christianity has not failed; it just has not been tried in many places. When all fails, we need to go back and read the directions. The key is to be Spirit-filled so that we might reproduce ourselves.

We Must Undertake the Requirements for Being Spirit-filled

The command from God is to be Spirit-filled; and everything that God requires of us, He also teaches us what to do. *Be filled with the Spirit* (Ephesians 5:18). Do not think of the Holy Spirit as a substance but as a person and refer to the Holy Spirit as Him: *But the Helper, the Holy Spirit, whom the Father will send in My name, He will teach you all things* (John 14:26). We must not depersonalize the Holy Spirit for He is a person and we are His temple. *Do you not know that your body is a temple of the Holy Spirit?* (1 Corinthians 6:19).

1. A complete commitment. To be filled with the Holy Spirit means to make a complete commitment to Him. We have opened the door of the temple, welcomed Him in, and given Him the key to every door and every room.

Many have said, "Holy Spirit, my body is Your temple. Come in and bless me and fill me and take control." However, is there any area in our life that is off-limits? Have we really given Him the key to every door—the keys to our business life, our dating life, our social life, and our financial life? There must be a complete commitment to the Holy Spirit; and to be filled with the Holy Spirit means, "Lord, I am committed to You."

When the burning ambition of our heart and life is to exalt the Lord Jesus and we have given Him the key to every door, then we are filled with the Holy Spirit.

The Holy Spirit has one ministry and that is to exalt the Lord Jesus Christ. When the burning ambition of our heart and life is to exalt the Lord Jesus and we have given Him the key to every door, then we are filled with the Holy Spirit.

2. A continual control. Ephesians 5:18 literally says, *Be filled with the Spirit.* That is the reason I previously asked the question: "Is the Holy Spirit filling you right now?" not "Have you been filled?" but "Are you being filled?" Why did He say, *Do not get drunk with wine, for that is dissipation, but be filled with the Spirit* (Ephesians 5:18) rather than "Don't steal but be filled with the Spirit" or "Don't commit adultery but be filled with the Spirit"?

Why did Paul take the particular sin of drunkenness and use it in contrast? Because being filled with the Spirit and being drunk with wine are antithetical. On the day of Pentecost, the Apostles were accused of being drunk with wine; and Peter said, *These men are not drunk, as you suppose* (Acts 2:15). They were not drunk with wine but with the Holy Spirit. God is using the Holy Spirit's fullness in comparison to drunkenness not only in contrast but also in comparison because being filled with the Holy Spirit is a lot like being drunk.

Being filled with the Spirit and being drunk with wine are antithetical.

Paul says, *Do not get drunk with wine . . . but be filled with the Spirit* (Ephesians 5:18). That is the problem with many people who have been Spirit-filled—they have sobered up. We need to be dependent upon the Holy Spirit continually.

There is a continual control where moment by moment we are saying, "Lord, I'm Yours."

3. A conscious claiming. We must claim this fullness by faith just as we received the Lord Jesus by faith. *Therefore as you have received Christ Jesus the Lord, so walk in Him* (Colossians 2:6). We then walk by faith simply by saying, "Lord, I open myself up and thank You that You are filling me right now. I claim the filling by faith—not by feeling." When we live in this way, we will be filled with the Holy Spirit of God.

We Must Utilize the Results of Being Spirit-filled

There are three basic results of being filled with the Holy Spirit, and they show up in all of our relationships in life: God, our circumstances, and other people.

1. In our relationship to God—a spirit of adoration. *Speaking to one another in psalms and hymns and spiritual songs, singing and making melody with your heart to the Lord* (Ephesians 5:19). We constantly want to be singing and praising the Lord, saying, "Jesus, I love You."

2. In our relationship to circumstances—a spirit of appreciation. *Always giving thanks for all things in the name of our Lord Jesus Christ to God, even the Father* (Ephesians 5:20). A Spirit-filled person is humbly grateful; a flesh-filled person is grumbly hateful.

A Spirit-filled person is humbly grateful; a flesh-filled person is grumbly hateful.

When we are filled with the Holy Spirit, we simply thank God for what He is doing in our hearts and lives. Paul does not say to give thanks "sometimes" but *always* nor does he say to "give thanks for some things" but *for all things*.

3. In our relationship to people—a spirit of accommodation. Paul wraps it up regarding our relationship to other people with a spirit of accommodation: *And be subject to one another in the fear of Christ* (Ephesians 5:21). Would life not be wonderful if we could just learn how to do that—if I could just submit to you and if you could just submit to me.

The key to success in our lives is the fullness of the Spirit, but the fullness of the Spirit is only to those who are under the control of the Spirit and submitted to the purpose of the Spirit. Submission — if we are not interested in the brakes, God is not going to show us the accelerator.

15

Our Work in Christ

There are three insights concerning what we call "the daily grind or Monday morning religion." *Slaves, be obedient to those who are your masters according to the flesh, with fear and trembling, in the sincerity of your heart, as to Christ* (Ephesians 6:5). The closest thing we would have to that is being obedient to a boss or superintendent.

We are to obey our boss as if he were Jesus. You say, "I don't believe it. That two-legged devil?" Yes, we are to serve *not by way of eyeservice, as men-pleasers, but as slaves of Christ, doing the will of God from the heart* (Ephesians 6:6) . . . *knowing that whatever good thing each one does, this he will receive back from the Lord, whether slave or free* (Ephesians 6:8).

We Have the Drudgery of Work

Our work is not always supposed to be exciting or thrilling or fun because there is a certain amount of work to work. God engineered it that way; He put some drudgery into all our lives and ordained it in the Garden of Eden after man's fall. *By the sweat of your face You will eat bread* (Genesis 3:19). However, there is a sense by which we can turn that boredom into blessing, that monotony into meaning, that drudgery into dignity, that grind into glory, and that rat race into a pilgrimage.

The problem with so many members in the church today is that we have divided our lives into the "secular" and the "sacred."

So many people feel insignificant and think, "If only I were a pastor, a missionary, or a minister of music or if I were wealthy, a politician, or a mover or shaker—but I am just an insignificant person. I don't have a lot of gifts or abilities; and very frankly, my job is quite insignificant also. I trudge to work every day and come back home. I really don't make a lot of difference. I'm locked in a job I despise but have to do it because it's the only job I can get. My life is totally unromantic and terribly unfulfilling with absolutely no dignity or real rhyme or reason to it. I do it simply because I have to."

However, we can turn drudgery into delight and monotony into something with great meaning. While we may think, "But it's secular work!" it really is not for there is no such thing as the secular and the sacred because the New Testament tells us how we can take what some would call secular and transform it into a sacred task. Our job can be our ministry, and our place of employment is the lampstand from which we let our light shine.

"But I'm only an ordinary person." God made mostly ordinary people and chooses to use mostly ordinary people that He might give them extraordinary power. When ordinary people do their work with extraordinary power, God is the one who gets the glory. "But I'm in an insignificant place." God takes ordinary people in insignificant places and uses them with extraordinary power for His glory.

Few have ever made it into *Who's Who*, a biographical dictionary of notable men and women; but each person is very important in the kingdom of God and has been called to a place of service to glorify the Lord.

The problem with so many members in the church today is that we have divided our lives into the "secular" and the "sacred." We live split-level lives, having the idea that we serve God part of the time and our secular employer part of the time. A man waits until he gets off work to go to the church where he can begin to serve God. He has a master on his job—the person he works for—and another master in the church—God. He is trying to serve two masters and *no servant can serve two masters* (Luke 16:13).

We must understand that when we are working a secular job, we are serving as though we were serving Jesus. It is not just working on an assembly line or checking out groceries or typing letters. It is a sacred task performed for the Lord Jesus Christ.

Many people, especially those in their thirties and forties who really get a good dose of old-fashioned salvation, come to the place where they make a full surrender to the Lord and say, "God, I want you to take control of my life and have every inch, every ounce, every nerve, and every fiber of me." Then, they begin to wonder, "Does

God want me to be a pastor? Does God want me to be a missionary? Does God want me to be an evangelist?"

If God calls them into the ministry, that is wonderful; however, we must never get the idea that some people are in full-time Christian service while others are not. There is no such thing as a Christian who is not in full-time Christian service. God wants people in full-time Christian service in every walk of life.

There is no such thing as a Christian who is not in full-time Christian service.

We Have Dignity in Our Work

The life of a child of God cannot be divided into the secular and the sacred because every day is a holy day, every place a hallowed place, and every deed a spiritual service.

A person who works a 40-hour week (and most people work more than 40 hours a week) and is not serving the Lord in their work because they do not see God in their work loses a quarter to a third of their time to an occupation where God cannot bless since they are not honoring Him. Are those 40 or perhaps 50+ hours wasted hours until they get off work and begin to serve God? No, because being a Christian is a full-time occupation. God does not have a duplex for a throne. We are not to serve God just when we get off work; we are to serve God 24-7.

Our lives are not like a pie where we give one-tenth to God and then we eat the nine-tenths or perhaps only give one-seventh of the pie to God and then do whatever we want with the rest. God does not have anything to do with that.

Every Christian works for God full-time even if their employment is with a secular company for *the earth is the Lord's, and all it contains* (Psalm 24:1).

Who was the first farmer? *The LORD God planted a garden toward the east, in Eden; and there He placed the man whom He had formed* (Genesis 2:8). God was the first farmer, not Adam. After God created the farm, He delegated the work to Adam. If Adam was taking care of the farm for God, he was doing the work of the Lord so it stands to reason that those who are farmers today are also doing the work of God.

> *With good will render service, as to the Lord, and not to men, knowing that whatever good thing each one does, this he will receive back from the Lord, whether slave or free* (Ephesians 6:7-8).

We do not work for a boss but for Jesus Christ; and knowing that whatever we do, we will receive the same from the Lord whether a slave or free. If we cannot do it as unto the Lord, we have no business doing it *knowing that from the Lord you will receive the reward of the inheritance. It is the Lord Christ whom you serve* (Colossians 3:24).

If a person works in a factory and puts caps on toothpaste, every cap is for Jesus. Whatever we do, we do as unto the Lord. A person does not have to play the piano in church or preach a sermon in order to serve God.

We Have the Duty of Our Work

God intended the church to go out, scatter, and permeate the community in the workplace. It is one of the most extraordinary opportunities we have to share the gospel of our Lord and Savior Jesus Christ. An example of that was a man named Daniel.

Daniel was taken to Babylon against his will. He did not go as a priest or a pastor or a music director or an educational director; but because of his extraordinary gifts, he was given a place of government service—a very important job working for King Darius.

If we find ourselves in a situation and there is nothing we can do about it and no other job is available, we must take it that we are there by the will of God.

In time, King Darius agreed to enforce an unchangeable injunction that whoever made a petition to any god or man besides him for thirty days would be cast into the lion's den. Daniel knew the document had been signed yet continued to kneel and pray and give thanks to God three times a day. When the king was informed of Daniel's continued prayer, he was deeply distressed and tried to rescue Daniel. However, a law of the Medes and Persians could not be changed, so he had Daniel cast into the lions' den. The king arose at dawn, and *when he had come near the den to Daniel, he cried out with a troubled voice. The king spoke and said to Daniel, "Daniel, servant of the living God, has your God, whom you constantly serve, been able to deliver you from the lions?"* (Daniel 6:20). It is worth noting that the king said to Daniel, "I know you serve your God continually."

Some say, "I don't even know that I'm in the will of God in my job. I don't have any sense of a call. The only reason I'm doing what I am is that it's the only job I could get. If I could get a better one, I would. I hate it, I'm not paid well, and I'm not maximizing my gifts. The only reason I'll go to work tomorrow is because I've got to feed my family. Like that bumper sticker says, 'I owe, I owe, it's off to work I go.'"

If we find ourselves in a situation and there is nothing we can do about it and no other job is available, we must take it that we are there by the will of God. *Thus says the LORD of hosts, the God of Israel, to all the exiles whom I have sent into exile from Jerusalem to Babylon* (Jeremiah 29:4). We often think that the king of Babylon caused the Jews to be carried away, but God said He caused it.

Though we may not have chosen where we are any more than Daniel would have chosen to go to Babylon, perhaps we are right where God put us. Perhaps our call is the call to captivity. Perhaps where we are living right now is our Babylon. Some may say, "Frankly, there's not much I can do about it. I just wish I could get out of here so I could serve God — perhaps in some monastery where I wouldn't have to have all these sinners around me."

That is not God's plan. God brought Daniel to Babylon because God had a purpose for him. We are not called to be an island of irrelevant piety surrounded by an ocean of need. God's plan for us is not to flee the world but to overcome the world.

This is Monday morning religion — how to turn a rat race into a spiritual pilgrimage. If we work in Babylon, *I do not ask You to take them out of the world, but to keep them from the evil one* (John 17:15). Jesus did not pray for our isolation; He prayed for our insulation.

In Paul's letter to Titus, he spoke concerning one of the Jewish converts who had become a Cretan prophet and had made a statement that *Cretans are always liars, evil beasts, lazy gluttons* (Titus 1:12). The Apostle Paul told Timothy that *for this reason I left you in Crete, that you would set in order what remains* (Titus 1:5). You do not take a lighthouse and put it in downtown Manhattan. You put it out on some barren, craggy, rocky shore where it is needed.

God placed Daniel in Babylon. He did not have what we would call "a full-time Christian service job." He was a bureaucrat. We have been saved out of this world and then sent back into the world as a witness. This is our main business for Jesus has called us to be *the light of the world. A city set on a hill cannot be hidden; nor does anyone light a lamp and put it under a basket, but on the lampstand, and it gives light to all who are in the house* (Matthew 5:14-15).

We are not called to be an island of irrelevant piety surrounded by an ocean of need.

We are the light of the world, not the light of the church. Our job is our lampstand—where we let our light shine *so that you will prove yourselves to be blameless and innocent, children of God above reproach in the midst of a crooked and perverse generation, among whom you appear as lights in the world* (Philippians 2:15). Our light is to shine in the midst of obscene stories, pornography, blasphemy, materialism, and gossip. We are called to let our light shine for the Lord Jesus Christ in the midst of a self-centered world.

Beloved, I urge you as aliens and strangers [that is what we are as this world is not our home] *to abstain from fleshly lusts which wage war against the soul. Keep your behavior excellent among the Gentiles so that in the thing in which they slander you as evildoers, they may because of your good deeds, as they observe them, glorify God in the day of visitation* (1 Peter 2:11-12). Our conduct is to be honorable among the Gentiles so that when they speak against us as evil doers—and they will, they will also see our good works and glorify God.

If we keep walking the straight and narrow and letting our light shine in the midst of a crooked and perverse generation where our job becomes a temple of devotion and our lampstand a witness, we will have a deep impact in the world.

Following are a few guidelines for success regarding our temple of devotion and the lampstand in our mind:

1. When at work, do not brag. Do not be self-righteous. There is nothing more obnoxious than a self-righteous person. *Let your light shine before men in such a way that they may see your good works, and glorify your Father who is in heaven* (Matthew 5:16). The shine should be a glow, not a glare. We must not go around talking and bragging about how good and righteous we are. No one has ever been won over to Jesus by this method.

2. When at work, do not nag. *Conduct yourselves with wisdom toward outsiders, making the most of the opportunity. Let your speech always be with grace, as though seasoned with salt, so that you will know how you should respond to each person* (Colossians 4:5-6). We must not nag people; and if we have an opportunity to witness, we should not be "preachy."

3. When at work, do not lag. On the job, we should carry our share of the load because it is a sin for Christians to do less than their best. The best workers in any setting should be children of God.

When employers go to an employment agency looking for workers, they ought to be able to say, "Here are my latest job descriptions. If you have any Christians, please send them to me because they are always on time; do not gossip, steal, or flirt around; and always treat me with the greatest of respect. Christians are the best people I have, and I want more."

We are not to be laggards. When we are paid to do a job, we should do that job because we are not doing it for the boss but for Jesus Christ.

It is a sin for Christians to do less than their best.

---

4. When at work, do not sag. We should never compromise our Christian walk but be righteous, clean, and pure. If we want people to believe in the faith we have, we need to go to work full of joy. The Apostle Paul tells us to *rejoice in the Lord always* (Philippians 4:4).

Jesus was a man of sorrows, but He was also a man of joy. *These things I have spoken to you so that My joy may be in you, and that your joy may be made full* (John 15:11). Some people arrive at work on Mondays with a hangover while others have just had a fight with their spouse. Many have been fighting traffic or cannot find a parking place, and half of them hate their jobs.

When Christians walk into a workplace, they should bring sunshine with them. Some will think, "What's the matter with him? What makes her so joyful?" However, when Christians are joyful week after week, the other workers will conclude that they have a supernatural life and will desire to know more.

Most people are not interested in heaven or hell; they just want to know how to get through Monday—how to get through life. Many of them have all kinds of problems and will eventually ask, "Where do you get your joy?

Sanctify Christ as Lord in your hearts, always being ready to make a defense to everyone who asks you to give an account for the hope that is in you, yet with gentleness and reverence (1 Peter 3:15).

When Christians walk into a workplace, they should bring sunshine with them.

When they ask what makes us different from everyone else, we will be able to answer, "If it were not for Jesus, I'd hate this job too; but I believe I am here by the providence of God and the Lord is the one who gives me songs in the night. I have heartaches, tears, and problems too; but Jesus has helped me and this same Jesus can help you too."

THE HORRIFIC BATTLES

16

Our Warfare in Christ

There is a dark, diabolical, deadly, dirty war that is being fought throughout the world. It is a form of guerilla warfare—sabotage, subversion, innuendo, sniping. It is a deadly war—a war between light and darkness, good and evil, heaven and hell, Christ and Satan. Whether we realize it or not, we are a part of this war. We cannot afford to be ignorant, and we cannot possibly be neutral. If we try to be neutral, we will find ourselves in the crossfire and in the most dangerous place of all.

> *Finally, be strong in the Lord and in the strength of His might. Put on the full armor of God, so that you will be able to stand firm against the schemes of the devil. For our struggle is not against flesh and blood, but against the rulers, against the powers, against the world forces of this darkness, against the spiritual forces of wickedness*

in the heavenly places. Therefore, take up the full armor of God, so that you will be able to resist in the evil day, and having done everything, to stand firm. Stand firm therefore, having girded your loins with truth, and having put on the breastplate of righteousness, and having shod your feet with the preparation of the gospel of peace; in addition to all, taking up the shield of faith with which you will be able to extinguish all the flaming arrows of the evil one. And take the helmet of salvation, and the sword of the Spirit, which is the word of God. With all prayer and petition pray at all times in the Spirit, and with this in view, be on the alert with all perseverance and petition for all the saints, and pray on my behalf, that utterance may be given to me in the opening of my mouth, to make known with boldness the mystery of the gospel, for which I am an ambassador in chains; that in proclaiming it I may speak boldly, as I ought to speak (Ephesians 6:10-20).

The Church is not a showboat but a battleship. We are at war; however, our call to arms is also a declaration of victory. When we were born again, we were born from above; and being heaven-born, we are heaven-bound. When we were born again, we were born to win.

The Christian Warrior and Our Adversary

We must know our adversary—our enemy. *Put on the full armor of God, so that you will be able to stand firm against the schemes of the devil* (Ephesians 6:11).

In our sophisticated age, we make the idea of a real and a personal devil more or less laughable. He is sometimes seen as a guy in long red underwear with a pitchfork trying to catch someone bending over. Others think of him as a medieval superstition. Football teams are called devils and demons, and we talk about deviled ham and devil's food cake. We make light of the devil, but he is our enemy.

He is not a figment of our imagination for it has always been his purpose to pull the veil of darkness over his kingdom and have his very existence denied for a season although he really does not want that because in the end, he desires worship. He will only use this disguise for so long before he removes the veil and says, "Bow down and worship me."

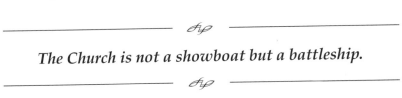

The Church is not a showboat but a battleship.

In our warfare, it is important that we understand who the devil is because if there is no enemy, there is going to be no preparation for war.

At Easter, we often sing: "He lives! He lives! Christ Jesus lives today! He walks with me and talks with me along life's narrow way." We could also sing about Satan: "He lives! He lives! Satan lives today! He wears on me and works on me along life's narrow way."

1. **Satan is a decided fact.** Those who do not believe the devil exists are in a very precarious situation.

2. **Satan is a destructive foe.** *So that you will be able to stand firm against the schemes of the devil* (Ephesians 6:11). The Greek word for "schemes" is *methodia* from which we get "methodical" or "method." Satan is very methodical and his warfare very ***strategic***. He may even take two steps back in order to go three steps forward. He may let us think we are getting away with sin and may even seem to bless us and help us along the way; however, he has

made a plan to sabotage our plans and our homes. The dynamite is in place, the fuse is laid, the match is struck, and Satan is working.

He is *strategic* but he is also **spiritual**. *For our struggle is not against flesh and blood, but against the rulers, against the powers, against the world forces of this darkness, against the spiritual forces of wickedness in the heavenly places* (Ephesians 6:12). People sometimes think that because something is spiritual, it is good. Not so. There is spiritual goodness as well as spiritual wickedness. *Beloved, do not believe every spirit, but test the spirits to see whether they are from God* (1 John 4:1).

Satan is *strategic* and *spiritual* and **strong**. We wrestle not against flesh and blood but against *principalities* and *powers* (Ephesians 6:12 KJV). In our flesh, we are no match for our adversary. We are too puny and weak to come against Satan in our own strength. We might as well be throwing snowballs at the Rock of Gibraltar.

Satan is *strategic, spiritual,* and *strong* but also **sinister**. Paul writes about *spiritual forces of wickedness in the heavenly places* (Ephesians 6:12). Satan has dark, devilish, tyrannical power and is going to fight to the finish. There is nothing he will not do to wreck, ruin, and destroy our lives. He knows he has but a little while and is like a cornered animal, fighting with no holds barred.

3. Satan is a defeated force. *Be strong in the Lord and in the strength of His might* (Ephesians 6:10) because our God has already defeated Satan—not that Satan shall be defeated but that he already is defeated.

Jesus said, *Now judgment is upon this world; now the ruler of this world will be cast out* (John 12:31). John wrote, *You are from God, little children, and have overcome them; because greater is He who is in you than he who is in the world* (1 John

4:4). Satan is strategic, spiritual, strong, and sinister; but God is greater than the devil who is in the world.

God presently allows Satan to have limited power on this earth but power that we as Christians can and shall overcome in the Lord Jesus Christ. Part of God's plan is to make us overcomers to give greater glory to Himself.

It is integrity that holds everything together.

The Christian and Our Armor

We not only need to recognize our enemy, but we also need to prepare for battle, for if we are not prepared, we will lose. We must put on the whole armor of God—holy armor. *Therefore, take up the full armor of God* (Ephesians 6:13) and *stand firm therefore, having girded your loins with truth* (Ephesians 6:14).

1. The believer's integrity. We are to put on the girdle of truth which is the believer's **integrity**. Truth stands for integrity. We often see motorcycle riders and weight lifters with leather belts around them that hold their loins together—their center strength. A Roman soldier wore a tunic with a leather belt—a girdle that was cinched tightly to prepare him for battle.

It is integrity that holds everything together. Truth and integrity are synonymous. We are to believe the truth, know the truth, love the truth, tell the truth, live the truth, and preach the truth. If we do not war with integrity, our lives will come apart.

Satan is a liar and will come against us with lies. His attack will bring a lack of integrity into our lives, but Jesus is the truth.

Are we wearing the girdle of truth or living a lie? If we are not wearing the girdle of truth, if we do not have integrity in our lives — in the big things and the small things — we are going to lose the battle. It is truth that holds everything together; without truth, everything falls apart.

2. The believer's purity. We are to wear the breastplate of righteousness which is the believer's **purity**. There is to be no unconfessed, unrepented sin in our lives. A Roman warrior had a breastplate that would have been made of woven chain to cover his heart, lungs, intestines, and vital organs. Without that breastplate, he was very vulnerable to arrows or a sword thrust.

Righteousness is purity. Jesus said, *Blessed are the pure in heart, for they shall see God* (Matthew 5:8).

The enemy wants to attack us not only with lies but also with impurity. He wants to get us to read filthy magazines and stay up late on Saturday nights watching filthy movies and then come to church on Sunday morning. He wants to get that filth into our hearts and minds. He wants to get us involved in crooked business deals. Satan knows where the crack in the armor is.

If our hearts are not pure before God, we will be defeated in battle because a piece of our armor will be missing; but Satan fears a holy Christian.

3. The believer's tranquility. We are to put on the shoes of peace which is the believer's **tranquility**: *having shod your feet with the preparation of the gospel of peace* (Ephesians 6:15). A Roman soldier would have hobnails on the bottom of his shoes — very much like football cleats — because when he was fighting, he needed to stand firm. Consequently, we need our feet to be shod with the preparation of the gospel of peace.

Paul is talking about peace with God and peace with one another. Satan comes against our integrity with lies and against our purity with lust. He puts stones and briars of doubts and discouragement into our lives in order to destroy our peace.

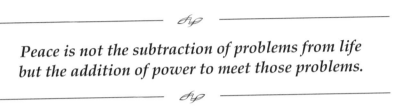

Peace is not the subtraction of problems from life but the addition of power to meet those problems.

If we have no peace, it is not because of circumstances. Peace is not the subtraction of problems from life but the addition of power to meet those problems. *Those who love Your law have great peace, and nothing causes them to stumble* (Psalm 119:165). The only way we can live in this manner is to put on the shoes of peace. Jesus made peace by His shed blood on the cross; and if we do not have this, we will slip and fall in battle.

Many believers do not fall because of a lack of integrity or purity but because of a lack of tranquility. Something will happen—sickness, disappointment, financial reverses, or a wayward child—and they lose their peace. We must put on the shoes of peace in order to be able to stand firm; otherwise, we will slip and fall.

4. **The believer's certainty.** We are to carry the shield of faith which is the believer's **certainty**. The Roman soldier's shield was about 2 feet by 4 feet and was made of wood covered with leather. The enemy would take flaming arrows, dip them in burning oil, and shoot them. With the flaming arrows flying back and forth, we are to take *up the*

shield of faith with which you will be able to extinguish all the flaming arrows of the evil one (Ephesians 6:16).

Satan uses lies so we put on integrity; he uses lust so we put on purity; and he will bring doubt and discouragement so we must put on tranquility. Then we must take up the shield of faith which is certainty. Satan is always shooting fiery arrows of doubt so we need the shield of faith to quench every fiery dart of the devil. We must feed our faith and starve our doubts.

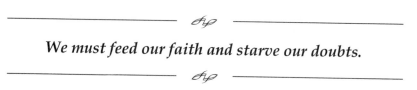

We must feed our faith and starve our doubts.

5. **The believer's sanity.** We are to wear the helmet of salvation which is the believer's **sanity.** *And take the helmet of salvation* (Ephesians 6:17). A Roman warrior would use a helmet to protect his head. It is a helmet of deliverance. It is having our minds under God's control.

A person without the Lord Jesus Christ has a form of insanity. Their minds are not what God made them to be. The helmet of salvation is our sanity, the covering for our minds.

We are now ready for battle. Each one of the pieces of armor represents Jesus. We must put on integrity, purity, tranquility, certainty, and sanity. Each piece is put on with prayer because what we are really doing is putting on the Lord Jesus Christ.

The Christian and Our Attack

It is not enough simply to put on the armor, but we also must get into the fight. What will guarantee our victory?

1. **The place of our stance.** *Therefore, take up the full armor of God, so that you will be able to resist in the evil day, and having done everything, to stand firm* (Ephesians 6:13).

Stand firm therefore (Ephesians 6:14). We have a place from which to fight because we stand in the victory that Jesus won at Calvary. *Be strong in the Lord and in the strength of His might* (Ephesians 6:10). We do not fight for victory; we fight from victory. We are to live life from a heavenly edge.

We are to live life from a heavenly edge.

---

2. **The power of our sword.** *And take the helmet of salvation, and the sword of the Spirit, which is the word of God* (Ephesians 6:17).

We have written about all of the protective armor. When we go into battle, it is necessary to wear a helmet and a breastplate and carry a shield; but it is vital that we have a sword. God has given us a place to stand and a sword with which to fight. The **power** of our sword is unlike any other sword—it is the sword of the Spirit. *For the word of God is living and active and sharper than any two-edged sword* (Hebrews 4:12).

Jesus had been fasting for forty days and forty nights and had become hungry. The devil came to Him and said, If You are the Son of God, command that these stones become bread (Matthew 4:3). Jesus then pulled out his "sword" and said, It is written, "Man shall not live on bread alone, but on every word that proceeds out of the mouth of God" (Matthew 4:4). On three occasions, Satan came to Him; and on all three occasions, Jesus replied, It is written. Jesus ran Satan through with that blessed blade all three times.

3. The provision of the Spirit. Once we take our place (dressed in the armor), we are standing in the finished work of Calvary. We take the sword of the Spirit which is the Word of God and then look to heaven for our supply. *With all prayer and petition pray at all times in the Spirit, and with this in view, be on the alert with all perseverance and petition for all the saints* (Ephesians 6:18).

When we go onto the battlefield, we stand in the finished work of Calvary.

Every warrior needs a supply and a commander in chief to guide and direct. When we go onto the battlefield, we stand in the finished work of Calvary. We take the Word of God which is the sword of the Spirit and offer our prayers to our heavenly commander, praying always with all prayer and supplication in the Spirit. It is the Spirit who directs our prayer and the Spirit who understands Satan's battleplan. Jesus is the one who knows how to wield and use the sword.

The Christian Warrior and Our Allies

We must unite forces. *With all prayer and petition pray at all times in the Spirit, and with this in view, be on the alert with all perseverance and petition for all the saints, and pray on my behalf, that utterance may be given to me in the opening of my mouth, to make known with boldness the mystery of the gospel* (Ephesians 6:18-19).

Paul was a warrior, but he knew he did not fight alone. He knew that we need to pray for one another because we fight the battle together. We are not a one-man army. If we stand alone, then we must fight alone. One could *chase a thousand, and two put ten thousand to flight* (Deuteronomy 32:30). There is a synergy that brings a divine energy when we fight together. We need each other and must lock arms, join forces, and fight together.

The church is a place where we reinforce ourselves and receive spiritual intuition, spiritual power, and spiritual encouragement in order to fight the battle because we fight with one another against a common enemy—not against one another.

- We are in a battle and must choose our side carefully because if we do not follow Jesus, we will be on the losing side.
- We must examine our hearts and make sure we have on the full armor of God.
- We cannot be neutral because this is a fight to the finish. Jesus said, *He who is not with Me is against Me* (Matthew 12:30).
- We can then rejoice and live victoriously every day.

Conclusion

We see the first heaven by day, the second heaven by night and the third heaven by faith. It takes faith to get to the third heaven. In 2 Corinthians 12:2, Paul specifically mentions the third heaven when he writes: "I know a man in Christ who fourteen years ago . . . was caught up to the third heaven."

The first heaven is the lowest level of heaven or simply the sky. It is the air we breathe as well as the different layers of the physical atmosphere surrounding the earth. It is the exosphere, thermosphere, mesosphere, stratosphere, and troposphere. It is the area of space that extends out away from the earth until it touches the solar wind, about 6.200 miles in altitude from sea level. In the Greek language, the same word for "heaven" is translated as "air." This is why we often see heaven referred to as things in the sky throughout the Bible.

The second heaven is what we often call "outer space." It's where we find all the sun, moon, stars, and planets in the universe. It is also called "celestial heaven." We read in Psalm 8:3-4, "When I consider your heavens, the work of your fingers, the moon and the stars, which You have ordained, what is man that You are mindful of him?

We also read in Matthew 24:29, "Immediately after the tribulation of those days the sun will be darkened, and the moon will not give its light; the stars will fall from heaven, and the powers of the heavens will be shaken." "And take heed, lest you lift up your eyes to heaven, and when you see the sun, the moon, and the stars, all the host of heaven, you feel driven to worship them and serve them" (Deuteronomy 4:19).

In this second heaven, also Scripture speaks of the "heaven of heavens." Though we don't know how far the universe extends, it seems the Bible is referring to its outer edges, where it is physical or metaphysical. We should read and ponder the Scriptures below:

"Indeed, heaven and the highest heavens belong to the Lord your God, also the earth with all that is in it (Deuteronomy 10:14).

"Praise Him, you heaven of heavens and you waters above the heavens!" Psalm 148:4).

"Behold, heaven and the heaven of heavens cannot contain You." (1 Kings 8:27).

In the first and second heaven is where Satan rules his evil empire with legions of demons and fallen angels. Demons have power. They have personality. They have purpose. Satan has come to rob, to kill and to destroy. If he can mislead you down a wrong path that will destroy your life's purpose . . . he has won the battle. The first and second heaven are his campground.

The Book of Ephesians was written to show us how to live the Christian life from a heavenly edge. We have the spiritual high ground for the battle of the ages; in the battle for the souls of countless numbers of people. Christ has given us the victory; now we have to walk by faith and claim it.

Then, there is the third heaven. Though a physical area cannot contain the Lord God due to His timeless nature, the third heaven is where He sits on His holy throne. It's His dwelling place, and it's where we will spend eternity in His presence and glory.

We read in Hebrews 8:1, "We do have such a high priest, who sat down at the right hand of the throne, the Majesty in heaven." In Acts 7:55, we learn, "But Stephen, full of the Holy Spirit, looked up to heaven and saw the glory of God, and Jesus standing at the right of God."

CONCLUSION

We are to "Give glory to your Father who is in heaven." (Matthew 5;16) "For Christ has not entered the holy places made with hands, which are copies of the true, but into heaven itself, now to appear in the presence of God for us." (Hebrews 9:24)

It takes faith in God to see and get to the third heaven.

We can look up and see the clouds and birds in the first heaven. We can build rockets to take us to the second heaven. However, there is only one way to get to the third heaven. As I said before, it takes faith in God to see and get to the third heaven.

There are mansions of splendor and robes that are dazzling white. The third heaven is our eternal home as children of the Most High God. It's the city where the Lamb is the light, where tears are never shed and good-byes are never uttered. There is no sorrow or pain, only joy and sheer perfection. It is the city where we will one day join the angels in singing, "Holy! Holy! Holy! Lord God Almighty!" around the throne of God. The third heaven is a real place with real people.

I love what we read in Hebrews 4:14-16: "Therefore, since we have a great high priest who has passed through the heavens, Jesus the Son of God, let's hold firmly to our confession. For we do not have a high priest who cannot sympathize with our weaknesses, but One who has been tempted in all things just as *we are, yet* without sin. Therefore, let's approach the throne of grace with confidence, so that we may receive mercy and find grace for help at the time of *our* need.

I encourage you not to miss it. We have a great high priest who has passed through the heavens. Can you see it? On the day of His ascension, Jesus went through the first heaven of the sky, the second heaven of the stars and to the third heaven where God dwells. In the Old Testament, the High Priest walked through the Outer Court, into the Holy Place, then through a thick blue tapestry embroidered with stars, he went into the Holy of Holies.

With the victory Christ has given to us, we don't have to prove anything, provide anything, or promise anything. We are called to live the Christian life from a heavenly edge!

Where are we to live our Christian life today? In the Holy of Holies; by faith in the third heaven. With the victory Christ has given to us, we don't have to prove anything, provide anything, or promise anything. We are called to live the Christian life from a heavenly edge!

About the Author and His Resources

Dr. James O. Davis is the founder of Cutting Edge International and Global Church Network, a growing coalition of more than 2,600 Christian ministries and denominations synergizing their efforts to build a premier community of pastors worldwide to help plant five million new churches for a billion soul harvest and to mobilize the whole body of Christ toward the fulfillment of the Great Commission. With more than 700,000 churches, the Global Church Network has become the largest pastors' network in the world.

Christian leaders recognize Dr. Davis as one of the leading networkers in the Christian world. More than 80,000 pastors and leaders have attended his biennial pastors' conference and leadership summits across the United States and in all major world regions. Dr. Davis is considered to be in the *Top Ten Christian Influencers in the World*.

In October 2017, Dr. Davis spearheaded and hosted *The Wittenberg 2017 Congress* in Berlin, Germany. The Wittenberg 2017 Congress celebrated the 500th anniversary of Martin Luther's nailing his 95 Theses on Castle Church door in Wittenberg, Germany. This historic congress brought together more than 650 influential leaders from more than 80 different denominations and every world region.

Dr. Davis served 12 years leading 1,500 evangelists and training thousands of students for full-time evangelism as the National Evangelists' Representative at the National Office of the Assemblies of God. Ministering more than 45 weeks per year for 40 years, Dr. Davis has now traveled over 10 million miles to minister face-to-face to millions of people in more than 130 nations.

Dr. Davis earned a Doctor of Ministry in Preaching at Trinity Evangelical Divinity School and two master's degrees from the Assemblies of God Theological Seminary.

Dr. James O. Davis' Books and Resources

- *We Are The Church: The Untold Story of God's Global Awakening* (coauthored with Dr. Leonard Sweet)
- *The Forgotten Baptism: Your Visionary Path To Success* (coauthored with Dr. Kenneth Ulmer)
- *The Faith Book: The Master Key To A Grand Life of Faith*
- *How to Make Your Net Work: Tying Relational Knots for Global Impact*
- *Scaling Your Everest: Lessons from Sir Edmund Hillary*
- *Gutenberg to Google: The Twenty Indispensable Laws of Communication*
- *The Great Commission Study Bible* (coauthored with Dr. Ben Lerner)
- *The Billion Soul Story*
- *12 Big Ideas*
- *The Pastor's Best Friend: The New Testament Evangelist*
- *Living Like Jesus*
- *The Preacher's Summit*
- *What to Do When the Lights Go Out*
- *It's a Miraculous Life!*
- *Signposts on the Road to Armageddon*
- *Beyond All Limits: The Synergistic Church for a Planet in Crisis* (coauthored with Dr. Bill Bright)
- *Winning Qualities Of High Impact Leaders*
- *The Adrian Rogers Legacy Collection*
- *The Ed Cole Legacy Collection*
- *The Elmer Towns Legacy Collection*
- *The Stephen Olford Preaching Collection*

His quotes and articles have appeared in scores of magazines, newspapers, and blogs.

Dr. Davis resides in the Orlando area with his wife, Sheri, and daughters, Olivia and Priscilla. They have two children, Jennifer, and James, who reside in heaven.

Notes

Notes

Notes

Notes

Notes

Notes